More Exciting, Funny, Scary, Short, Different, ... Like

...nce,

...ngs

Edited by

CARROLL

BEACHAM

...ndon 1992

Cover and text designed by Natalie Wargin

Composed by Precision Typographers in Palatino
on a Miles 33 Phototypesetting system

Printed on 50-pound Glatfelter, a pH-neutral
stock, and bound in 10-point C1S cover
stock by Edwards Brothers

The paper used in this publication meets the minimum requirements of
American National Standard for Information Sciences—Permanence of Paper for
Printed Library Materials, ANSI Z39.48-1984. ∞

Library of Congress Cataloging-in-Publication Data

Carroll, Frances Laverne, 1925–
    More exciting, funny, scary, short, different, and sad books kids
like about animals, science, sports, families, songs, and other
things / by Frances Laverne Carroll and Mary Meacham.
        p.   cm.
    Includes index.
    ISBN 0-8389-0585-4
    1. Children's literature—Bibliography. 2. Bibliography—Best
books—Children's literature. 3. Children—Books and reading.
I. Meacham, Mary, 1946–   .
Z1037.C294   1992
[PN1009.A1]
011.62--dc20   92-11588

Printed in the United States of America.

96 95 94 93   5 4 3 2

TO *Rosemary Margaret Meacham-Zittel*

Contents

Preface

MORE EXCITING, FUNNY, SCARY, SHORT, DIFFERENT, AND SAD BOOKS KIDS LIKE ABOUT ANIMALS, SCIENCE, SPORTS, FAMILIES, SONGS, AND OTHER THINGS is an annotated bibliography of the children's books that librarians recommend in answering children's requests for books. The title is appropriate because this bibliography is arranged in divisions that reflect the way children phrase their requests for books: for example, "I want a book about . . ."; "I have read . . . and want another like it"; and "I like to read about . . . ." We found this to be a unique and desirable arrangement when we were designing a format in 1983 for the first publication of this bibliography, and we feel that it is still a good way to entice children to read the popular books recommended by librarians. MORE EXCITING, FUNNY, SCARY, SHORT, DIFFERENT, AND SAD BOOKS KIDS LIKE ABOUT ANIMALS, SCIENCE, SPORTS, FAMILIES, SONGS, AND OTHER THINGS contains numerous and varied lists of children's books for children to use. The short, annotated selected lists of fiction and nonfiction books were submitted by practicing children's librarians. Not only the titles but also the subjects reflect the children's preferences as determined by the librarians. This edition is intended to serve as a companion to the previous edition, since there is a very small percentage of duplication of titles, and the new edition contains many new titles that have been published since 1983. It can also stand on its own since it includes the books children really *like*, regardless of the date of publication.

COMPILATION

For the new edition of EXCITING, FUNNY, SCARY, SHORT, DIFFER-
ENT, AND SAD BOOKS KIDS LIKE ABOUT ANIMALS, SCIENCE, SPORTS,
FAMILIES, SONGS, AND OTHER THINGS, our method of gathering information was similar to that used in the first edition. With the
assistance of Sue Galloway, Children Services Consultant, Oklahoma Department of Libraries, Oklahoma City, and Nan Sturdi-
vant, Children's Coordinator, Tulsa City-County Library, Tulsa,
Oklahoma, we again selected names from the membership list of
the Association for Library Service to Children (ALSC) of ALA and
contacted these people in order to learn directly from librarians the
favorite works of children. The lists of books could be of any length,
from five to fifteen books, and we reserved the right to add or delete
any book.

This book is unique in that the scope covers approximately
seventy-five topics that librarians know interest children and for
which they recommend these titles spontaneously. The topics have
been generated by the titles that librarians are using in response to
the children's requests. Inevitably, changes in these topics occur
over the years, and these changes have produced interesting lists
for this book. However, to suggest that a major trend in children's
reading interests has occurred is beyond the scope of this book.
When the survey was completed, we considered that our effort was
sufficient to determine whether children really ask for books on
these subjects and how they ask for them. We reminded the contributors that it was important to supply an annotated list of books that
they often currently recommend to children.

We reviewed each list to ensure that, in its totality, it is a fair
representation of the topic and will be comprehensible and appealing to children. We also reviewed each annotation to determine that
the language is natural to the children for whom the book is intended
and that it possibly presents new terms that will motivate children
to read. The contributors were asked to include fiction and nonfiction titles in a list if possible, and the lists remain mixed, without
any concern for a balance between the two.

Some titles appear on more than one list and have different annotations. In compiling the book, however, we followed a rather
strict policy of elimination in order to avoid a popularity contest between a few of the titles. The title and the annotation had to seem to
be the best suited for inclusion on a specific list and were eliminated
when they were marginal to that list. The number of titles on a list by

the same author was also monitored, and the titles were culled to be sure the author was included for the title best suited to that particular list. The remaining titles by that author were omitted, with the reasoning being that the bibliography will introduce children to authors or series, and they can then use it to get at other good books by the authors they especially like. The usefulness and scope of the book are increased considerably in this way, with the amount of bibliographic data minimized.

ARRANGEMENT AND CONTENT

This book is for children, and the arrangement of topics is indiscriminate. From a child's point of view, the topics do not need to be rigorously designated. As will be seen from the table of contents, children's interests often cannot be narrowly stated. The arrangement does not imply that the first lists contain the most popular topics. Within the lists the arrangement is alphabetic by title to attract those children who are not as yet familiar with very many authors.

The annotations are written in a brief, original, and popular style that stresses the aspects of the book that appeal to children. Emphasis is on books for children in the second to fifth grades. A few lists and books that are popular with the young but independent reader who appreciates some guidance in choosing titles are also included. The maximum upper range is the eighth grade, as the intent is to cover children's, but not young adult, books. The majority of the lists, however, do not contain any books that would reach this level.

PURPOSES

MORE EXCITING, FUNNY, SCARY, SHORT, DIFFERENT, AND SAD BOOKS KIDS LIKE ABOUT ANIMALS, SCIENCE, SPORTS, FAMILIES, SONGS, AND OTHER THINGS should be a valuable book for parents, teachers, librarians, and children. It does not attempt to provide an overwhelming number of titles nor a lengthy treatment of each title.

It is recommended for school-aged children to use as a personal reading guide.

In establishing a publisher and date of publication for each book, we made every attempt to supply a reliable source for obtaining a copy of the book, although the purpose of this publication is not to provide librarians with a buying guide. The bibliographic information nearly always refers to the hardback edition, and the date to its first edition, although many of these titles are also available in paperback. Very few titles are out of print, but it seemed obvious to us as we looked at the submitted lists that librarians were using working collections that contain some out-of-print books children still read and love. We therefore included out-of-print titles, deeming this to be valuable information.

There is a growing trend to become more aware of children's choices of books. This trend is evident in the state awards to authors based on children's voting for a favorite author. In addition, the responses that librarians make to children's requests are often expressed in the promotional brochures prepared especially by the children's departments of public libraries for distribution to parents, teachers, and children. This book follows this trend by attempting to provide, in an appealing format, a longer, convenient, and usable listing of titles that recognizes children's interests.

We are very grateful for all the assistance given by the librarians who submitted topics and prepared annotated lists.

FRANCES LAVERNE CARROLL
MARY MEACHAM

Acknowledgments

We especially wish to acknowledge the assistance of the staff of the Pioneer Multi-County Library, Norman, Oklahoma; Access Services of the Bizzell Memorial Library of the University of Oklahoma, Norman; and Susan Houck, Information Processing Center, University of Oklahoma, Norman. They kept us supplied with books to read and clean manuscript copy to edit.

We wish to thank the contributors for responding with topics, annotated lists, and suggestions. They are:

Bette Ammon
Missoula Public Library
Missoula, Montana

Jean Andres
Tippecanoe County Public Library
Lafayette, Indiana

Natalie Baldwin
Northwest Area Children's
    Coordinator
Northwest Regional Library
Philadelphia, Pennsylvania

Kathleen Behrendt
Berwyn Public Library Systems
Berwyn, Illinois

Christine Behrmann
Office of Children's Services
New York Public Library
New York, New York

Symme Benoff
Henderson District Public Library
Henderson, Nevada

B. Blakeman
Campbellsville Elementary Library
Campbellsville, Kentucky

Mary Frances Burns
Palatine Public Library District
Palatine, Illinois

Serena Butch
Head of Children's Room
Schenectady County Public
    Library
Schenectady, New York

Terry Lee Caruthers
Branch Manager
Burlington Branch Library
Knox County Public Library
    System
Knoxville, Tennessee

Rosalind Chang
San Francisco Public Library
Civic Center
San Francisco, California

Children's Staff
Sparks Branch
Washoe County Library
Sparks, Nevada

Barbara Clark-Greene
Children's Librarian
Groton Public Library
Groton, Connecticut

Sybil Connolly
Library Media Specialist
Windsor Hills Elementary School
Putnam City, Oklahoma

Marcia Conrad
Orange Public Library
Orange, Texas

Linda Cowan
Library Media Specialist
Harry S Truman Elementary
   School
Norman, Oklahoma

Elizabeth Danley
Youth Services Librarian
Pasco County Library System
Hudson, Florida

Mary D'Eliso
Children's Librarian
Monroe County Public Library
Bloomington, Indiana

Georgene DeFilippo
Coordinator, Youth Services
Bethel Park Public Library
Bethel Park, Pennsylvania

Sally Dow
Ossining Public Library
Ossining, New York

Carol Elbert
Ames Public Library
Ames, Iowa

Davi Jones Evans
Children's Program Librarian
Morgan Hill Library
County of Santa Clara
Morgan Hill, California

Ellen Fader and Staff
Westport Public Library
Westport, Connecticut

Judy Fink
Urbana Free Library
Urbana, Illinois

Linda Glawatz
Children's Program Librarian
Gilroy Public Library
Gilroy, California

Ruth Gleason
Media Coordinator
St. Charles School
Bloomington, Indiana

Beth Graham
Children's Librarian
Mission Branch Library
San Francisco Public Library
San Francisco, California

Donna Grossman
Children's Librarian
Schenectady County Public
   Library
Schenectady, New York

Joanne P. Grumman
Children's Librarian
Bethel Public Library
Bethel, Connecticut

Susan Harbaugh
Troy-Miami County Public Library
Troy, Ohio

Jane Harrington
Norman, Oklahoma

Barbara G. P. Hartley
Head, Children's Services, and
   Staff
Pioneer Multi-County Library
Norman, Oklahoma

Dorothy Jeffers
Librarian
Madison Elementary School
Norman, Oklahoma

Julianne Johnson
Ponca City Library
Ponca City, Oklahoma

Susie Jones
Hoxie School District No. 46
Hoxie, Arkansas

Susan Knorr
Children's Librarian
Zablocki Library
Milwaukee Public Library System
Milwaukee, Wisconsin

Alveeda Lauscher
Department Head, Children's
    Library
Salt Lake City Public Library
Salt Lake City, Utah

Dianne Lawson
Tippecanoe County Public Library
Lafayette, Indiana

Selma K. Levi
Head, Children's Department
Enoch Pratt Free Library
Baltimore, Maryland

Jill L. Locke
Department of Library and
    Information Studies
University of North Carolina
Greensboro, North Carolina

Lin Look
Manteca Library
Branch of Stockton-San Joaquin
    County Library System
Manteca, California

Marian Lytle
Children's Services Supervisor
Rowan Public Library
Salisbury, North Carolina

Deesha Martin
Children's Librarian
Milford Public Library
Milford, Connecticut

Phyllis McLaughlin
Morgan Hill Library
County of Santa Clara
Morgan Hill, California

Beverly Winters Moon
Coordinator of Children's Services
Phillipsburg Free Public Library
Phillipsburg, New Jersey

Linda A. Morris
Dayton, Ohio

John Peters
Epiphany Branch
New York Public Library
New York, New York

Jane Piggott
Tippecanoe County Public Library
Lafayette, Indiana

Pat Poulter
Arlington Public Library
Arlington, Texas

Karen Rehard
Children's/Young Adult Librarian
Missoula Public Library
Missoula, Montana

Cynthia K. Richey
Head of Children's Services
Mt. Lebanon Public Library
Pittsburgh, Pennsylvania

LaVonne Sanborn
Instructor, Department of Media
    and Educational Technology
Western Illinois University
Macomb, Illinois

Gale W. Sherman
Early Childhood Librarian
Pocatello Public Library
Pocatello, Idaho

Mary Kay F. Shives
Troy-Miami County Public Library
Troy, Ohio

Pamela L. Sidnell
Children's Librarian
Paris Public Library
Paris, Texas

Janice Smuda
Project LEAP Librarian
Cuyahoga County Public Library
Cleveland, Ohio

Anitra T. Steele
Mid-Continent Public Library
Independence, Missouri

Lillian Ashley Swain
Jackie Lewis, Dee Dallman, Laurie
   Sudo, Sandy Gilbert and
   Michaela Wayler
Virginia Beach Public Library
Great Neck Area Library
Virginia Beach, Virginia

Linda Tashbook
Children's Librarian
West End Branch
Carnegie Library of Pittsburgh
Pittsburgh, Pennsylvania

Virginia A. Tashjian
Library Director
Newton Free Library
Newton, Massachusetts

Nancy Titolo
Children's Librarian
Queens Borough Public Library
Jamaica, New York

Julie Tomlianovich
South-Central Kansas Library
   System
Hutchinson, Kansas

Merryl Traub
Head, Children's Services
Syosset Public Library
Syosset, New York

Suzanne Tynemouth
Malden Public Library
Malden, Massachusetts

Gloria Waggoner
Children's Librarian
Fair Oaks-Orangevale Community
   Library
Sacramento Public Library
Fair Oaks, California

Paige Gushikuma Wagner
Youth Services Librarian
Bud Werner Memorial Library
East Routt Library District
Steamboat Springs, Colorado

Debbie Watson
Librarian
Ysleta Independent School District
El Paso, Texas

S. Wilkie
Coordinator, Children's Services
Farmington Community Library
Farmington Hills, Michigan

Youth Services Department
Alachua County Library District
Gainesville, Florida

I Want a Twisted Folktale

Emily and the Enchanted Frog, by Helen V. Griffith. Greenwillow, 1989.

Emily kisses a frog suspecting she is doing some prince a great favor; but when the prince appears, he is totally ungrateful. The second story in this book is a version of *Three Wishes,* in which an elf grants Emily her one wish—to be invisible. In the third tale, a hermit crab emphatically insists to Emily that he is a mermaid.

A Frog Prince, by Alix Berenzy. Holt, 1989.

A frog admires a princess and quite willingly retrieves her golden ball from a swamp, but she isn't appreciative and laughs at him, so he sets out to find a more suitable mate. His search is hindered by two trolls and a green-faced witch but assisted by a dove and some turtles. This new ending to a traditional tale borrows elements from other tales, including the kiss that awakens a sleeping princess. You will love the illustrations and giggle over a frog who blushes a deep green.

Jim and the Beanstalk, by Raymond Briggs. Coward, 1970.

Like Jack, Jim awakens one morning to find a great plant growing outside his window. Like Jack, he climbs it and discovers a castle. The giant who lives in the castle, however, assures Jim there is nothing to fear, because the giant is old and hasn't any teeth. He can't read, either, because of poor eyesight, and feels embarrassed about his bald head. Jim goes up and down the plant retrieving new glasses, new false teeth, and a wig of flaming red hair.

Prince Cinders, by Babette Cole. Putnam, 1987.

Prince Cinders, who is not handsome and very skinny, dreams of being big and hairy like his three brothers. Then a fairy accidentally turns him into a big, hairy monkey! He doesn't know this and sets off for a dance. At the stroke of midnight he turns back into his old self but loses his trousers while being chased by a beautiful princess. She uses his jeans, which no one else can get into, to catch him.

The Principal's New Clothes, by Stephanie Calmenson. Scholastic, 1989.

Hans Christian Andersen's *The Emperor's New Clothes* has been modernized to include the town's sharpest dresser, Mr. Bundy, the school principal. Two tailors promise him an amazing suit made from special cloth "that is invisible to anyone who is no good at his job or just plain stupid." Mr. Bundy ends up wearing only his *A-B-C* boxer shorts in front of a school assembly, until a kindergarten child tells the truth. Other students save the day for Mr. Bundy.

Sidney Rella and the Glass Sneaker, by Bernice Myers. Macmillan, 1985.

While his older brothers go off to football practice, poor Sidney Rella is always left behind to do the housework. His wish for a chance to try out for the football team is overheard by a fairy godfather, who magically does all the housework and who—after failing the first time—finally produces the appropriate uniform, complete with *glass* sneakers.

Sleeping Ugly, by Jane Yolen. Coward, 1981.

Princess Miserella is beautiful, but mean and worthless. Lost in the forest, she meets Plain Jane, a poor orphan who is a kind person—so kind that she uses up two of her own wishes to undo spells that an ugly old woman, a fairy in disguise, has cast on Princess Miserella. All three of them end up with a one-hundred-year nap, but only two of them are kissed awake by a prince.

Snow White in New York, by Fiona French. Oxford, 1986.

Snow White lives in New York, where her stepmother is the Queen of the Underworld. A bodyguard has been ordered to shoot Snow White but just can't do it, leaving her lost and alone. Seven jazzmen adopt her; and when her singing debut hits the front page, her stepmother tries again to get rid of her—with a poisoned cherry in a cocktail!

The True Story of the 3 Little Pigs, by A. Wolf, as told to Jon Scieszka. Viking, 1989.

We finally have an opportunity to hear the wolf's side of the story. Alexander T. Wolf wasn't looking for a pig to eat; he was trying to borrow sugar to make his dear old granny a birthday cake. He didn't huff and puff the house down on purpose—he huffed and snuffed and sneezed because he had a bad cold.

I Like Stories with Computers in Them

Chip Mitchell and the Case of the Stolen Computer Brains, by Fred D'Ignazio. Dutton, 1982.

Join Chip, as in "computer chip," in solving ten thorny cases that involve cheating by computing and erratic computer behavior. You'd better know your computers first! Solutions are included in the back of the book.

The Computer Nut, by Betsy Byars. Viking, 1984.

Katie's new computer friend has a—literally—unearthly sense of humor. When Kate is contacted through her father's computer by someone claiming to be an alien, she can't decide if it's for real or not. If so, what will happen if BB-9 keeps his promise and meets her at Big Burger? Is someone playing a trick on her? She teams up with her friend Willie, and together they solve this funny mystery.

The Computer That Ate My Brother, by Dean Marney. Houghton, 1985.

Harry gets an unusual computer for his twelfth birthday: It can read his mind. The trouble begins when Harry *thinks* he'd like to get rid of his big brother Roger, who is trying to steal his computer. The screen says *Stop! Warning! Stop!* Then the computer and Roger disappear. Later the computer reappears on its own, but Roger's return is left open to debate.

The Computer That Said Steal Me, by Elizabeth Levy. Four Winds, 1983.

All of Adam's new friends have computer chess games. He

can't afford to buy one of his own so he figures out a plan to steal one. It's a perfect plan—or so he thinks—but he's nervous even before he goes into action. His feelings then are nothing compared to what he experiences once he starts on his plan and finds the consequences more than he can bear.

The Ghost Squad Breaks Through, by E. W. Hildick. Dutton, 1984.
Wacko and Buzz, Danny, Joe, Karen, and Carlos make a great team of detectives—especially since the last four are ghosts! How do the dead members communicate with the living? By computer, of course. By micro-micro-microwaves, to be exact, which can go to anyone with instruments sensitive enough to detect them.

The Great Gradepoint Mystery, by Barbara Bartholomew. Macmillan, 1983.
Ricky and his computer-club friends are working very hard to keep up their grades so they can win a very large amount of money, offered as an achievement prize, for their school. Someone, however, is using a computer to lower their marks and stop them from winning. Then, Ricky teams up accidentally with ALEC (Access Linkage to Electronic Computer). While he watches people at the schools, ALEC searches the data bases. Together they come up with two suspects: the school janitor and the computer club adviser at a rival school.

Miss Pickerell and the War of the Computers, by Dora F. Pantell. Watts, 1984.
A power-hungry computer programmer has plans to take over Square Toe City, and only the heroic Miss Pickerell stands in his way. She decides to investigate the high prices of the supermarket that is using the new bar codes, which her nephew, Euphus, who knows all about computers, has explained to her. He also suggests the means to rescue her from a mountain cable car in which the programmer has trapped her.

Do You Have Any Books about Climbing a Tree?

A B C E D A R, an Alphabet of Trees, by George Ella Lyon. Watts, 1989.

Trees give us air, food, shade, wood, and—especially—something to climb. Not only are these twenty-six trees arranged alphabetically by name but the size and shape of each, along with its leaf and fruit, are also shown.

The Girl Who Would Rather Climb Trees, by Miriam Schlein. Harcourt, 1975.

Melissa receives a doll from her family, and she knows they think she should be glad; but she really doesn't like dolls. She has to find a creative way to satisfy her family and still get outside to climb trees.

The Giving Tree, by Shel Silverstein. Harper, 1964.

The life of a boy and that of a tree he loves are intertwined. From a place to climb in his youth to a stump to rest on in his old age, the tree provides him with the things he needs and wants, because the tree loves him.

I Wish I Had a Big, Big Tree, by Satoru Sato. Kaisei-sha, 1984.

Kaoru wishes for a tree, then dreams of all the wonderful things he would do if he had one: for instance, climbing inside the tree to his kitchen to make pancakes and climbing outside to his lookout. He tells his father about it, and they work out a solution.

When Dad Cuts Down the Chestnut Tree, by Pam Ayres. Knopf, 1988.

All the great things Dad could make from the wood of the chestnut tree—not to mention the fun of playing on the trunk— at first appeal to the children. Then they decide these are not as important as having a place to play, to swing, to hang a birdhouse, and to enjoy other nice activities.

Got Any Good Science Books? With Lots of Pictures?

Dive to the Coral Reefs, by Elizabeth Tayntor, Paul Erickson, and Les Kaufman. Crown, 1986.

Like a great undersea city, the coral reef teems with plants and animals, from those you can barely see to huge, toothy sharks and barracudas. Take a tour through this exotic land with a team of expert divers from the New England Aquarium via the gorgeous color photographs.

Exploring the Titanic, by Robert D. Ballard. Scholastic, 1988.

The famous story of the *Titanic*'s first—and last—voyage is told by the modern explorer who found its wreckage at the bottom of the ocean in 1985. The largest ship of its time, this ocean liner hit an iceberg in the North Atlantic on April 14, 1912, sending hundreds to their deaths. In 1986, Ballard and his team went down to explore the sunken liner. They used a sonar vehicle, a deep-towed camera, and a remote-controlled underwater robot, all of which are described in this book.

Giants of Land, Sea and Air, Past and Present, by David Peters. Knopf, 1986.

Just how big do elephants, whales, and sharks really get? Which was larger: Allosaurus or Tyrannosaurus? Here you can see most of them on colored fold-outs, along with giants that you have never heard of and several smaller animals that you have—including us! The same scale for showing size is used for all.

The Hidden Life of the Pond, by David M. Schwartz. Crown, 1988.

The photographs are a complement to the text and a colorful window on the many plants and animals found in and around the pond—from frogs to raccoons, from tiny bloodsucking mosquitoes to graceful deer.

Jupiter, by Seymour Simon. Morrow, 1985.

The earth is very far from Jupiter, and our first pictures of Jupiter were made in 1977 from unmanned Voyager spaceships. The color pictures were taken thirty-two million miles away from Jupiter because a spaceship cannot survive if much closer than that. The planet remains practically unknown and seemingly very unlike the earth in its composition.

The Magic School Bus at the Waterworks, by Joanna Cole. Scholastic, 1986.

Let Ms. Frizzle, the teacher, be your guide as you and your classmates follow the water you drink—into the sky, down below the earth, and all the way into the sinks of your school bathroom! There are three kinds of colored drawings: comic-book balloons, pages from a school notebook, and informative labels and signs, wherever you and your group go.

Skeleton, by Steve Parker. Knopf, 1988.

Color photographs and drawings, small and large, are all over the pages. They entice you to look at large, small, heavy, and hollow bones, showing you what bones are made of and how they work together in human and animal skeletons.

Do You Have Any Books like The Baby-Sitters Club?

Aurora and Socrates, by Anne-Catharina Vestly. Crowell, 1969.

Aurora and her baby brother Socrates are used to having Daddy take care of them while their mother goes to work; but when Daddy needs to spend more time at the university finishing his degree, they have a succession of baby-sitters, including Gran (who isn't really their grandmother and has never ridden on an elevator before), Uncle Brande, Granny, and her friend Patten. Through it all, they manage to have many exciting adventures, such as when Aurora's friend Brit-Karen hides in the closet so she won't have to move to a different apartment building or when Patten and Socrates, pretending to be cows, get locked in a cattle car on a train.

Baby-Sitting Is a Dangerous Job, by Willo Davis Roberts. Atheneum, 1985.

Darcy is frightened when she and the Foster children are kidnapped, but she is terrified when she accidentally identifies the kidnappers. They are the family of a girl in her class, and she knows that now they won't let *her* go! She and the children must escape. First they must charm the Doberman dogs, which Shana, who is two-and-a-half, begins instinctively to do. Melissa is four and too scared to be of much help; but Jeremy, who is six, joins Darcy in a three-pronged escape plan that they know has little chance of working.

Goldenrod, by Mary Towne. Atheneum, 1977.

A baby-sitter who answers an ad to care for five children every afternoon from three to six o'clock—even though she meets only some of the requirements (she has a car and likes to play games but has no references)—turns out to be exceptional. Goldenrod is her name, and she can transport the children to a chosen place anywhere in the world and get them home on time. When Mrs. Madder discovers this wonder, she goes, too. Each has a chance to choose before the game (the book) is finished and Goldenrod leaves.

Ginnie and Her Juniors, by Catherine Woolley. Morrow, 1963.
Too young to baby-sit! Ten-year-old Ginnie is tired of being told that. But is she ready to handle five kids—preschoolers, at that? Geneva agrees to help her for a share of the baby-sitting money but doesn't seem too elated. Ginnie thinks Geneva might like baby-sitting better when Geneva has more experience!

Henry Reed's Baby-Sitting Service, by Keith Robertson. Viking, 1966.
To make money over the summer, Henry decides to try baby-sitting, since that's what people in Grover's Corner need most. Of course, he didn't reckon on a little girl with a habit of constantly disappearing, on terrible screams at five in the morning when he and one of the children camp out, or on losing a mobile home during lunch! In the end, however, he and his assistant Midge Glass receive an award for their contribution to the community.

Katie's Baby-Sitting Job, by Martha Tolles. Scholastic, 1985.
It is Katie's first baby-sitting job, and she is excited and pleased about it, until she sees an empty jewelry box and reports it to the Stellans when they return home. They call the police immediately. Katie realizes that she may never be asked to sit again and that the police suspect her.

Taking Care of Terrific, by Lois Lowry. Houghton, 1983.
When fourteen-year-old Enid (who prefers to be called Cynthia) agrees to baby-sit with four-year-old Joshua (who prefers to be called Tom Terrific), she envisions a few pleasant summer days on Boston Common. Then they decide, with the help of a saxophone player from the park, to organize some of the street people to picket the Popsicle stand for not selling root-beer Popsicles. All goes well, but then, joined by Enid's friend Seth, they decide to "borrow" the swan boats for a midnight ride; and suddenly, they are in more trouble than they bargained for.

The Ten-Speed Baby-Sitter, by Alison Cragin Herzig and Jane Lawrence Mali. Dutton, 1987.
Tony is left alone in a summer cottage with three-year-old

Duncan when Duncan's mom takes an unexpected weekend trip. Tony will receive a bonus; and since all this happens immediately upon his arrival to baby-sit for a month, he doesn't have time to anticipate the problems. Tremaine, the girl who does the lawn and wants to be a biologist, helps him. Tony's bicycle gets them to the beach, and they find a green egg to incubate. Unfortunately, a storm cuts off the electricity; and Tony has extra problems when the egg hatches, burglars arrive, and Duncan's mom's plane is delayed.

Tough-Luck Karen, by Johanna Hurwitz. Morrow, 1982.

Karen hates the move from New York City to New Jersey. She's shy and doesn't make friends or do well in school. At her first baby-sitting job, her family drives her crazy by calling to check on her every few minutes. She continues to baby-sit with two-year-old Keith Collins, helps her brother with his fifth grade history project, and really enjoys cooking. It is the last that brings her success, and making bread for her science project saves her school grade.

Where Can I Find Books about the People of Asia?

A Chinese Zoo, Fables and Proverbs, by Demi. Harcourt, 1987.

Thirteen fables relate Chinese traditions, and pictures of the main characters—hedgehogs, pandas, deer, cats, birds, unicorns, and others—appear in the book on an open fan. The one-line moral at the end of each fable is in English and Chinese.

Count Your Way through China, by Jim Haskins. Carolrhoda, 1987.

Haskins employs the same idea for two books, this one about China (the other about Japan). He uses the numbers one through ten to illustrate important facts about Chinese history, geography, government, customs, music, work, animals, and achievements. Each number is written in Chinese and followed by its pronunciation in Mandarin, the official language of the People's Republic of China.

The Crane Wife, retold by Sumiko Yagawa. Morrow, 1981.

A poor young peasant removes an arrow from the wing of a crane and, that night, mysteriously acquires a beautiful young wife who is wondrously skilled at weaving. He obeys her admonition not to watch her while she works at her loom. Later, impelled by greed, he asks her to weave; and, overcome by curiosity, he opens the door and faints at the sight. His crane-wife sorrowfully wings her way back to her own people, lost to him forever.

The Eternal Spring of Mr. Ito, by Sheila Garrigue. Bradbury, 1985.

Sara, a young British war evacuee living in British Columbia, is befriended by her uncle's gardener, Mr. Ito. When internment of the Japanese-Canadians is ordered, he is unwilling to be imprisoned. Sara comes to understand his choice of death and its manner, and she later smuggles the valued ancient family bonsai to Mr. Ito's interned family.

Girl from the Snow Country, by Masako Hidaka. Kane/Miller, 1986.
      The snow is very deep this year—soft and fluffy—when Mi-chan and her mother walk to the village market. On the way Mi-chan stops to brush the snow from the statue of Jizo, protector of children and travelers. When they arrive at the market, she sees the flower stall, and, remembering that the snow bunnies she has made at home need eyes, she wonders if she can afford a branch with some berries.

Hiroshima No Pika, by Toshi Maruki. Lothrop, 1980.
      Seven-year-old Mii is living in Hiroshima on August 6, 1945, the day the atomic bomb is dropped. She goes with her mother, who carries Mii's father to the river. They see death and tremendous damage everywhere after the explosion. After four days they find shelter, then a hospital for her father. She and her mother return, but Mii finds only her rice bowl, bent and broken. What happens to them in the years afterward is equally bleak.

Lon Po Po, a Red Riding Hood Story from China, translated by Ed Young. Philomel, 1989.
      Three little Chinese girls outwit a wolf who is posing as their grandmother, who comes to visit them when their mother is not at home. They are suspicious, and Shang, the eldest, is clever. A basket and gingko nuts are involved, but the basket is used quite differently in this tale.

Park's Quest, by Katherine Paterson. Dutton, 1988.
      When is it time to know about your ancestry and who is to tell you? When he is almost twelve, Park decides that he wants to know about his father, who was killed in Vietnam. His mother won't tell him enough but permits him to visit his grandfather, the colonel; his Uncle Frank; and Thanh, a girl his age. They give him an insight which leaves his father almost *less* real to him.

The Tongue-Cut Sparrow, retold by Momoko Ishii. Dutton, 1987.
      An old man loves a sparrow as a pet and is richly rewarded. His cruel and greedy wife mistreats the sparrow but still thinks that if she finds the home of the tongue-cut sparrow, she will receive riches. Her gift is in a basket, which she must not open until she is home. It is heavy and must be a treasure, she reasons. What is inside cures her of greediness, they say.

Do You Have
Any Scary Books?

FUNNY AND A LITTLE SCARY

The Blossoms Meet the Vulture Lady, by Betsy Byars. Delacorte, 1986.
Junior Blossom has just finished making a coyote trap. He is setting his trap in the woods, and it snaps shut on him. When he does not return home that night, his family begins a frantic search for him, all to no avail because he has been discovered by Mad Mary, the vulture lady, an old recluse who carries him to her cave deep in the woods. People know her but not where the cave is!

In a Dark, Dark Room, and Other Scary Stories, retold by Alvin Schwartz. Harper, 1984.
The author's advice is to tell these stories in front of a fire in the dark, *s-l-o-w-l-y* and quietly, and have fun. Some of the seven are scarier than others but not so scary as to give you nightmares.

My Friend the Vampire, by Angela Sommer-Bodenburg. Dial, 1985.
Tony loves vampire movies and books, but he hadn't bargained on a real vampire appearing in his room one night. Furthermore, this vampire, a boy about his own age, has a little sister who thinks Tony is wonderful. They *seem* friendly, but what if they suddenly remember they are vampires who drink blood! Tony is also having trouble keeping all this from his parents, as the vampires come to visit him more and more often.

My Parents Think I'm Sleeping, poems by Jack Prelutsky. Greenwillow, 1985.
His parents may think he's asleep, but the little boy in these poems has found all kinds of things to do besides sleeping! Some

are fun, some are a little scary; and sometimes he actually falls asleep.

The Secret Life of Dilly McBean, by Dorothy Haas. Bradbury, 1986.

Dilloway (Dilly) seems an average boy. He gets along fairly well in school and camp with others his age, and his grades are okay. In reality, however, he is an orphan who is sent by his bank to private schools and has a strange gift that he tries to hide: magnetically sensitive hands. When Dilly is given a bicycle, a dog (and what a crazy dog Contrary is), and a home of his own (with servants), life seems even better. Others observe all of this, and it is the actions of two mysterious groups of good and bad gals and guys who upset his own thoughts about how to use his talent.

The Whipping Boy, by Sid Fleischman. Greenwillow, 1986.

Young Prince Brat and Jemmy, his whipping boy (the prince has a stand-in for whippings), are kidnapped as they run away from the royal palace. Held for ransom by Cutwater and Hold-Your-Nose Billy, two unsavory scoundrels, they can't agree on tactics, but they escape by running to a safe place—the rat-infested sewers! They must still confront the king and face their punishment, and Prince Brat makes some big promises.

SCARY

Bony-Legs, by Joanna Cole. Four Winds, 1983.

Because of her kindness to a witch's dog and cat, Sasha is able to escape being eaten by terrible Bony-Legs. The animals give her a mirror (a lake) and a comb (a fence of trees), which magically defeat the witch who is chasing her.

The Gunniwolf, retold by Wilhelmina Harper. Dutton, 1946.

Little Girl's mother tells her always to stay close to home, but one day Little Girl goes to pick flowers, happily singing kum-kwa, khi-wa; and before she knows it, she is in the middle of a jungle. The gunniwolf sees her and chases her—hunker-cha, hunker-cha, hunker-cha.

King of the Cats, a Ghost Story, by Joseph Jacobs, retold by Paul
　　Galdone. Houghton, 1980.

　　The black cat, Old Tom, listens intently from the lap of the
gravedigger's wife as her old man excitedly tells her about a band
of nine cats that came in a procession carrying a coffin to the graveyard to bury their dead king. They were led by a cat that looks like—
their own black cat!

Scare Yourself to Sleep, by Rose Impey. Barron's, 1988.

　　Camping out in a tent in the yard, two girls tell each other
scary stories as a game. The winner is the one who goes to sleep
first. After one falls asleep, the other hears a tap-, tap-, tapping on
the tent. Is it the invisible man, the wind, or Simon, who is their
age? While the other one continues to sleep, they (it was Simon) eat
up the food and intend to tell her when she awakes it must have
been the invisible man, of course.

Wiley and the Hairy Man, adapted from an American folktale, by
　　Molly Garrett Bang. Macmillan, 1976.

　　The horrible hairy man who lives in the swamp near the Tom-
bigbee River is after Wiley. Wiley's dogs are not much protection,
but Wiley manages to get away twice in the swamp. When the hairy
man comes to the house to get Wiley, it's a good thing Wiley's
mother is one smart woman.

I Want to Be Really Scared

Behind the Attic Wall, by Sylvia Cassedy. Crowell, 1983.

When twelve-year-old Maggie goes to live with her aunts and an uncle, she is expecting to have a very boring time. When she sees the house, she thinks she's been tricked into going to yet another boarding school which she knows will be horrible. She hears voices in the massive stone house. To whom do they belong? What do they want? Maggie is a disappointment to her aunts, so she is sent away again, but she goes knowing for the first time what it means to leave something and someone she loves.

The Castle in the Attic, by Elizabeth Winthrop. Holiday, 1985.

William uses a magic token to shrink himself and the housekeeper, Mrs. Phillips, to the size of the toy knight that inhabits the castle she plans to give him before her return to England. Now they join in a challenging quest to break the spell of an evil magician. William must go through the training of a squire and seek out the castle of Alastar and look into the eyes of the dragon that guards its gates.

Christina's Ghost, by Betty Ren Wright. Holiday, 1985.

Uncle Ralph doesn't believe ten-year-old Christina when she tells him that she has seen the ghost of a little boy and thinks there's another presence in the old house where they're staying. He is taking care of Christina while her grandmother is in the hospital, and it is a long time before he says she is a "rare one" and means it as a compliment. When he sees the ghost, they try to solve an old crime together.

Deadly Stranger, by Peg Kehret. Dodd, 1987.

Twelve-year-old Shannon is kidnapped by David, who once lived in her house when he was a child. He is a mental patient recently released to a halfway house and now reported missing. David confuses Shannon with Angie, his sister. Shannon's friend Katie, who has only recently moved to the town, witnesses the kidnapping and realizes she too is in danger.

The Dollhouse Murders, by Betty Ren Wright. Holiday, 1983.

Amy is glad when Aunt Clare asks her to stay with her in the old family farm house. However, she is mystified by a dollhouse she finds in the attic, because something seems to be happening to the dolls every time she goes near. Amy is both frightened and curious. Louann, her brain-damaged younger sister, goes with her to the attic during a storm; and Aunt Clare is grateful for the letter they find there that explains some real murders.

The Eyes of the Amaryllis, by Natalie Babbitt. Farrar, 1977.

When Jenny arrives at Gran's to help out since Gran has a broken ankle, she feels an immediate attraction for the ocean, which she has never seen before. When it comes time to leave, she is sad, having seen the ocean in many moods. In what seems to her an incredibly short time, she encounters a ghost; hears the story of the sinking of the *Amaryllis* in 1850 and how it affected the family; joins Gran in her vigil of over thirty years, waiting for a sign from the sea; and experiences a hurricane. Most of the time it is scary and uncomfortable; yet she is glad that Gran and her father are planning to repair Gran's house, because she will then be able to return.

Haunted Island, by Joan Lowery Nixon. Scholastic, 1987.

Determined to build a retreat on the lovely island adjoining her inn, Aunt Jennie finds that the local men refuse to work there because they think the island is haunted. Chris and Amy set off in a leaky boat with ghostly Amos Corley, who has told them about the island, to "put the ghosts to rest." He goes off mysteriously, leaving them with a boat that is now too leaky for a return trip, and they encounter the ghost and his ghost dog. They are glad to be rescued after they unravel the mystery that they doubt their aunt will believe.

The House with a Clock in Its Walls, by John Bellairs. Dial, 1973.

Lewis Barnavelt likes his uncle's house and his first evening there; something puzzles him, however. They cannot find the source of a strange ticking, and the house is burgled for what looks like a clock key! Who needs a key, if the clock has been ticking for years in his Uncle Jonathan's house? Then other things begin happening. What evil has been freed by Lewis's incantation and thoughtless prank in the cemetery?

If You Want to Scare Yourself, by Angela Sommer-Bodenburg. Lippincott, 1989.

Freddy has already been confined to his bed for two weeks with a sore leg—and it hasn't healed yet! He asks his mom, dad, and grandmother to tell him scary stories. He learns that Harry, his father's math tutor, was really a vampire. His mother tells about her Aunt Matilda, who worked for a family that had a maze that should never be entered alone. Eventually, Freddy creates his own scary story to tell his parents. It is really scary.

More Scary Stories to Tell in the Dark, by Alvin Schwartz. Harper, 1984.

A dead man comes back for his murderer; so does a little black dog. A butcher makes special sausage, while a town mysteriously loses its children, puppies, and kittens. You can even find instructions for conjuring up a ghost in your very own bathroom mirror; only be sure to keep your hand on the light switch just in case! This is a horrendous collection of terrifying tales and haunting illustrations to keep you up at night.

The Mysteries of Harris Burdick, by Chris Van Allsburg. Houghton, 1984.

If you read a lot of scary stories, your imagination starts to play tricks on you when you're at home alone in bed, when the floors creak, or when the wind shrieks around your house and you forgot to shut your window. If you can dream up stories when the sheets are over your head at night, you can surely spark a story, a really scary story, from these fourteen pictures with only titles and captions.

The Oracle Doll, by Catherine Dexter. Macmillan, 1985.

Gabriella, the talking doll that Lucy gets for her birthday, turns out to be an oracle who predicts the future. Lucy, her older sister Rosy, and their neighbor James form a close friendship while guarding the secret of this special doll. After the doll is stolen by some envious friends, strange Mr. Edgar comes to the rescue, using a lineup of look-alike dolls. It is Rosy who realizes that he wants the real doll so that he can return it to Delphi. She does not want to know her future but has loved being in on something special, and they strike a bargain.

Something Upstairs, a Tale of Ghosts, by Avi. Orchard, 1988.

Kenny Hulsdorf's family moves from California to a historic old house in Providence, Rhode Island. Kenny claims the attic for his own, but he soon finds out that he is not the only resident. He notices a stain on the floor, which turns out to be human blood. One night Kenny hears a scraping noise and sees hands that rise from the stain and move aside a box of his mother's books. Eventually, the entire body of a young black man emerges from the stain. It is Caleb, a slave, who asks Kenny to help him find his murderer. Decide for yourself who is haunting whom.

Wait Till Helen Comes, a Ghost Story, by Mary Downing Hahn. Clarion, 1986.

Heather stumbles on a girl's forgotten grave, and the ghost of the girl, Helen, visits her. Heather feels strangely attached to her. What does Helen want? Can Heather help, or will she be Helen's next victim? Heather's half-brother Michael and his sister Molly are accused of dividing the family, while they think it is the fault of Heather and Helen. Helen plays an active role in the reconciliations!

Where Are
the Dinosaur Books?

Big Old Bones, a Dinosaur Tale, by Carol Carrick. Clarion, 1989.

When the train stops for water on their trip west, Professor Potts and his family walk about. When he finds a very large, very old bone, he decides to stay and dig until he has lots of bones to take back east to assemble. Before he shows this strange animal to scientists from around the world, he has his wife make a skin for it. Tribrontosaurus rex is truly amazing.

Cam Jansen and the Mystery of the Dinosaur Bones, by David A. Adler. Viking, 1981.

Three bones are missing from the tail of the museum's dinosaur. Cam remembers what it looked like on a previous visit, and Eric buys a postcard of the dinosaur skeleton that proves the bones are missing. Caught after hours in the museum, Cam is not believed by the director when he tells him why he and Eric are there. Cam has to look for other clues in order to find the thieves—and the reason anyone would want dinosaur bones!

Dinosaur, by David Norman and Angela Milner. Knopf, 1989.

When you open this treasure of pictures and stories, you will feel a dinosaur detective's delight. In two-page sections you will discover why dinosaurs' tails were long, why their skins were tough, when they lived, what they ate, and how we find out about them. Tidbits of myths and legends about these great creatures end the book.

Dinosaur Bones, by Aliki. Crowell, 1988.

Dinosaurs lived approximately sixty-five million years ago,

but the first recorded discovery of a giant fossil bone was in 1676. In the 1800s, Mantell, Owen, Marsh, and Cope found more bones and speculated or proved what *Dinosauria* (terrible lizards) were; what conditions supported their growth; and what happened to cause their extinction. Scientists today continue to add to this information.

Dinosaur Cousins? by Bernard Most. Harcourt, 1987.

Is it possible? Could it be? Do dinosaurs have relatives that exist today? This is a convincing and humorous argument about the possibility that dinosaurs are the ancestors of some modern-day creatures. According to the author and his pictures, the habits and body parts of ancient dinosaurs are similar to those of many of today's favorite wild animals that we see in zoos. It is certainly something to think about.

Dinosaur Dig, by Kathryn Lasky. Morrow, 1990.

Max and Meribah are two lucky kids. Their family gets to go on a real dig for dinosaurs in the Badlands of Montana. They learn all about the methods paleontologists and their helpers use to uncover Tyrannosaurus rex and Triceratops. Heat, grit, small bones, and patience are the order of the day, until the diggers are rewarded by finding the rib of a Triceratops.

Dinosaur Mountain: Graveyard of the Past, by Caroline Arnold. Clarion, 1988.

In 1909, Earl Douglass, a paleontologist, discovered a mountain ridge in Utah that eventually yielded fossils of ten different kinds of dinosaurs, including the most complete apatosaurus skeleton ever found. Today, this area is a national park called Dinosaur National Monument, where visitors can see fossilized dinosaur bones still embedded in the rock and watch scientists painstakingly removing these and other fossilized remains dating to 145 million years ago. It is about as near the real thing as you can get.

Draw 50 Dinosaurs and Other Prehistoric Animals, by Lee J. Ames. Doubleday, 1977.

Each page has a picture of a dinosaur, identified by its name and length and accompanied by a descriptive phrase. The drawing starts with a circle, oval, or other simple shape, to which are added a few lines—and a few more lines—until a full picture of a dinosaur emerges. You are encouraged by the author to follow these steps carefully until you can draw with ease and confidence—and later creatively.

A Gallery of Dinosaurs and Other Early Reptiles, by David Peters. Knopf, 1989.

If you've ever wondered what a particular dinosaur looked like, how big it was, what it ate, or when it lived, this is the place to look. All dinosaurs, including little-known ones, are fully described; and many of them are illustrated. Pre- and post-dinosaur ages are included, and some information is pinpointed by geographic area—North America and Mongolia, for example.

If You Are a Hunter of Fossils, by Byrd Baylor. Scribner, 1980.

For the fossil hunter, the present recedes and the past becomes more real, in the imagination, than the here-and-now. A whole drama is played out in your mind as you examine a rock or a bone.

Last Dinosaur, by Jim Murphy. Scholastic, 1988.

A female Triceratops is traveling with two male Triceratops, and they encounter fires, an angry male Tyrannosaurus rex, and a raging river. She protects her nest of eggs until she is forced to make a quick decision to save herself.

My Daniel, by Pam Conrad. Harper, 1989.

Julia, eighty years old, tells her grandchildren, Ellie and Stevie, about a time when she was twelve and she and her brother Daniel found a dinosaur on their farm in Nebraska. She has come for the first time to see the assembled sixty-seven foot Brontosaurus. As the three of them stand before it, she finishes the story, telling them why one toe is missing and where it is—their secret.

Nate the Great and the Sticky Case, by Marjorie Weinman Sharmat. Coward, 1978.

Claude collects stamps with dinosaurs on them, and he's missing his Stegosaurus stamp, so he asks Nate to find it. Nate interviews the suspects and goes to the museum to see a Stegosaurus. Thinking of the other side of a stamp, which is sticky, Nate wonders who was out in the rain before the stamp was missed. Aha! Now to find the shoe.

The New Illustrated Dinosaur Dictionary, by Helen Roney Sattler. Lothrop, 1990.

The title explains what this book is—a reference tool arranged alphabetically by dinosaur names, with related subjects included in the listing. The introductory pages and a map give information about the major ages of prehistoric life millions of years ago. The pronunciations and sources of the dinosaur names are included with the entries, as are some cross-references and illustrations, where appropriate. An appendix carries the geographic references further.

The News about Dinosaurs, by Patricia Lauber. Bradbury, 1989.

Brontosaurus has a new head—one the proper size; and there are four new kinds of dinosaurs: Baryonyx, Mamenchisaurus, Deinonychus, and Nanotyrannus. Scientists are busy comparing today's reptiles and everything they know now about dinosaurs and coming to new conclusions.

What Happened to Patrick's Dinosaurs? by Carol Carrick. Clarion, 1986.

While he is raking leaves with his older brother Hank, Patrick asks him where the dinosaurs went and doesn't agree with his brother's explanation. Patrick thinks the dinosaurs built homes, cars, and roads for people because they were big and strong; and when they got tired of working for people, they built a spaceship for themselves!

Do You Have Any Books about Birthdays?

The Birthday Burglar and a Very Wicked Headmistress, by Margaret Mahy. Godine, 1988.

In the first of these two stories, Bassington discovers he has never had a birthday and decides to steal a few. He orders the butler to get out the hot-air balloon and the black burglar suit that belonged to Great-Uncle Brinsley. The butler warns him that birthdays are not as easy to get in this manner as bicycles, for example, and thinks no good will come of this.

The Birthday Moon, by Lois Duncan. Viking, 1989.

These rhymes show you many beautiful, tantalizing, and extraordinary things you can do in your imagination if you ever receive the moon or half of it or even a sliver for a birthday present!

Everyone Else's Parents Said Yes, by Paula Danziger. Delacorte, 1989.

Matthew is counting down (5 days, 15 hours, and 32 minutes) to a major sleep-over party for his eleventh birthday, but he has problems. Big problems! Someone—really eleven someones—is out to get him with green Jell-O in his desk and a note from the Get-Him Club (Girls Eager to Halt Immature Matthew). This is prebirthday; what will they do on his birthday?

The Half-Birthday Party, by Charlotte Pomerantz. Clarion, 1984.

Busy preparing for Katie's birthday party, Daniel forgets his own instructions to the guests: Be prepared to tell a whole story about a half-present, since his sister is six months old. They wonder what Daniel will bring! So does he! He is the last one to give his present, a super gift to be seen when it gets dark.

Handtalk Birthday, by Remy Charlip and Mary Beth and George Ancona. Four Winds, 1987.

Learn some sign language as you enjoy Mary Beth's birthday party and guess with her what is inside all of her packages, how well she likes them, and how old she is.

Happy Birthday from Carolyn Haywood, by Carolyn Haywood. Morrow, 1984.

All the people in this book are having birthdays. Betsy is eight, and Jonathan Mason is six when they celebrate their birthdays. The party for Mr. Kilpatrick, the policeman, turns out well, even though Billy accidentally sits on the cake.

Lucky Charms and Birthday Wishes, by Christine McDonnell. Viking, 1984.

Emily's lucky charm is working well, so far. She's making friends in the new term at school. Her birthday party is also great, but she did not get what she wanted. Will she when her grandmother comes? It isn't what you think; it's better—the ending, that is.

So You Want to Plan a Birthday Party! by Catherine A. Durkin, Sally A. Willette, and Ann D. Wyles. Atheneum, 1980.

You have a hand in planning and giving great birthday parties in this book that includes all the steps of preparation, for different ages and groups or by themes, games, or crafts. Recipes are included.

Staying Nine, by Pam Conrad. Harper, 1988.

Heather has had a wonderful time being nine, but her birthday is near; can she stop herself from turning ten? Being ten involves a lot of things: less climbing of walls, more attention to clothes and hair. She doesn't want a birthday party, so an unparty is her next choice. However, when she changes her mind, it's like New Year's Eve; exactly at 7:45, she is ten. What changed her mind?

I Only Want One That You Like

All-of-a-kind Family, by Sydney Taylor. Follett, 1951.

Ella is the oldest of five girls, and there hasn't been a new baby for five years. Will it be a "her"? Gertie, the youngest, isn't sure she wants any. Papa gets what he wants; and after the baby arrives, it is not an all-of-a-kind family anymore that lives on New York's lower East Side in 1913.

Anansi and the Moss-Covered Rock, retold by Eric A. Kimel. Holiday, 1988.

A magic moss-covered rock causes all who comment on it to fall asleep. A trickster spider named Anansi uses the rock to fool all the animals in the forest—all but one—in order to pick from their food his favorite things to eat. Little Bush Deer is cleverer than Anansi and fairer to the other animals, and he wants to teach Anansi a lesson. Do you think Anansi the spider learns?

Are All the Giants Dead? by Mary Norton. Harcourt, 1975.

James decides to stay with the two Jacks (Jack-the-Giant-Killer and Jack-of-the-Beanstalk) at the pub they operate now that they are older, while Mildred goes to a wedding at the castle. He describes Mildred as slightly silvery and says that she is always writing in her notebook because she reports events to people such as Beauty and the Beast, Cinderella, and Sleeping Beauty. Princess Dulcibel runs off, and James decides to help her find the talisman that will break the spell cast by Pinprickel, the bad witch. An ugly, smelly giant has it! The two Jacks assist. Then James hears a car door slam.

The Fledgling, by Jane Langton. Harper, 1980.

Six-year-old Georgie wants to fly like a downy seedling from a milkweed pod. When she senses she has been recognized by a large Canada goose, she lets the goose carry her, floats free, and is caught on his sturdy back again. Even her eccentric family says no more of that and takes steps to stop her and her Goose Prince.

The Great Book Raid, by Christopher Leach. Warne, 1979.

King Arthur drives a Rolls Royce. Tarzan works in a traveling circus. Long John Silver lives in the Happy Harbour Nursing Home. Are these men the heroes of some of Jim's favorite children's books? Yes. Or imposters? Well, no. Are they needed to squash the new plans for a hotel on the beach? It helps. Is there more to this? Yes. Jim understands after their weekend at his home.

It All Began with Jane Eyre; or, the Secret Life of Franny Dillman, by Sheila Greenwald. Little, 1980.

Franny loves to read *Jane Eyre,* but her mother thinks she should be reading modern teen books that deal with everyday problems, stories that will not cause her imagination to run wild. After reading four such books and deciding to keep a journal as had the four girls in the stories, she discovers what must be exciting events— that she has not noticed—in the lives of her family and their friends!

The Lemming Condition, by Alan Arkin. Harper, 1976.

Every ten years or so thousands of lemmings jump off cliffs and fall into the ocean. The problem is lemmings do not swim. Only one lemming realizes this and attempts to find out why everyone wants to go—why even he wants to go—especially after he purposely goes into water and knows what it is like. What can he do to break the pattern of his species, which is unique in its march to the west?

Roger's Umbrella, by Honest Dan'l Pinkwater. Dutton, 1982.

Roger doesn't like his umbrella very much, because it misbehaves and always gets him in trouble. It takes him up several times, and one very windy day it carries him across town and drops him in the backyard of three old women. They teach him how to talk to an umbrella and give him some tea and cookies. You might like to know the words Roger now uses with his umbrella.

Tuck Everlasting, by Natalie Babbitt. Farrar, 1975.

Would you want to live forever? A young girl must make that

decision after meeting the Tuck family, in which no one ever ages, gets sick, or dies. Her knowledge jeopardizes their way of life, unless she goes with them, and she likes them very much.

Wilfrid Gordon McDonald Partridge, by Mem Fox. Kane/Miller, 1985.

He has four names and isn't very old, and he lives next door to an old people's home. He knows everyone there, but his favorite person is ninety-six-year-old Miss Nancy Alison Delacourt Cooper, probably because she has four names, too. Wilfrid helps Miss Cooper find her memory.

I Want a Story like Cinderella

The Egyptian Cinderella, by Shirley Climo. Crowell, 1989.

Rhodopis is a Greek slave whose master doesn't hear his servants tease her and order her about; but he does see her dance one day. He decides to reward this gift of dance with dainty leather slippers, the toes of which are gilded with rose-red gold. A falcon steals one slipper and drops it in the Pharaoh's lap; he declares that the owner shall be his queen. The search of the old tale is on!

Moss Gown, by William H. Hooks. Clarion, 1987.

When Candace, the third daughter of the house, declares that she loves her father more than meat loves salt, she is misunderstood; and he gives possession of his land to her two older sisters, forcing her to leave. Candace is found by a gris-gris woman who gives her a magical moss gown, and Moss Gown becomes her name. She hides the gown and later wears it to the young master's ball, but it turns to rags at daylight. He searches the countryside for the beautiful stranger. Eventually he finds her; and she finds her father, who admits he misjudged her.

Princess Furball, retold by Charlotte Huck. Greenwillow, 1989.

To avoid an unwanted marriage, a beautiful princess runs away wearing her coat of a thousand furs. After being found by a king's hunter, she becomes a kitchen servant. The night of the king's ball, she transforms herself into a foreign princess so that she may attend. A gold ring, a good thimble, a little gold spinning wheel, and the king's favorite soup all help uncover her disguise.

Tattercoats, an Old English Tale, told by Flora Steel. Bradbury, 1976.

Because his favorite daughter died giving birth, the old lord refuses to even look at his granddaughter. She is barely fed and clothed; hence, her name—Tattercoats. Her only friend is a goose-herd who owns a magical pipe. It is this pipe that helps the prince fall in love with Tattercoats and transforms her rags into a beautiful gown.

Yeh-Shen, a Cinderella Story from China, by Ai-Ling Louie. Philomel, 1982.

After her jealous stepmother stabs her pet fish, Yeh-Shen discovers that its bones contain magic—enough magic to furnish food so she can live, and enough to provide beautiful clothes for a festival. Her fish, however, won't speak to her when she loses one golden slipper. While Yeh-Shen searches for the slipper, the king searches for the woman who fits the slipper.

Do You Have Any Books about Aliens?

Aliens for Breakfast, by Jonathan Etra and Stephanie Spinner. Random, 1988.

Richard finds Aric, Commander of the Interspace Brigade, in his cereal called Alien Crisp. He joins Aric in his fight to stop Dorf, one of the space monsters called Dranes, capable of dividing and multiplying, that move in to destroy earth. The weapon is a food that Aric remembers in time!

The Computer Nut, by Betsy Byars. Viking, 1984.

BB-9 is an alien from Iaxtron, where intelligent beings can fly. He also thinks he is a comedian. He and Kate, the computer nut, communicate, at first by computer and then in person!

Earthlets as Explained by Professor Xargle, by Jeanne Willis. Dutton, 1988.

Preparing his class for a peaceful tour of the planet earth, Professor Xargle explains the odd life of earthlets (human babies), which the aliens will discover on their visit. They can be recognized by their roar, he says.

The Long Blue Blazer, by Jeanne Willis. Dutton, 1987.

Wilson is a new kid in school, very short and very quiet. Isn't it odd that he will never take off his long blue blazer? Wilson seems to belong to no one and has a ready answer to any question. A schoolmate asks him home and is astonished when, that night, a spaceship comes to pick Wilson up. Now we know why he didn't take off his blazer.

Stinker from Space, by Pamela F. Service. Scribner, 1989.

Tsyng Yr has important information to deliver to his planet, but the enemy disables his scout ship. He has to land on another planet, earth; and he is injured. He must find an appropriate host-body quickly—a skunk's will do. Karen, whose sandwich attracts the skunk, and Jonathan, who has a computer, help him return to his planet, a feat that involves Stinker—that's his new name—in chemical warfare and space-shuttle hijacking.

The Trouble with Gran, by Babette Cole. Putnam, 1987.

The senior citizens do not suspect Gran is an alien. When they take a trip to the seashore with a group of school children as part of a school's project, she livens up the fun fair and acts up in general. They make an unscheduled side trip to her home planet, after she turns the bus shelter into a spaceship!

UFOs, ETs and Visitors from Space, by Melvin Berger. Putnam, 1988.

Over the years, many people have seen unidentified flying objects and what they believed to be aliens from outer space. In most cases, these sightings turned out to have commonplace, earthly explanations. In a few cases, however, there is the possibility of extraterrestrial visitation. The sheer size of the universe makes it unlikely that earth is the only inhabited planet, and the government is making efforts to contact beings on other planets, who probably have a more advanced civilization than ours.

Do You Have Any Pop-up Books?

The Car and Truck Lift-the-Flap Book, by Gerard Browne. Lodestar, 1989.

The working parts of each vehicle are revealed or uncovered by lifting layers of flaps, and the parts are labeled. Cars and trucks used for a variety of everyday purposes are shown. Within each grouping, additional models are illustrated.

Hide and Seek. National Geographic Society, 1985.

Three-dimensional scenes of the forest, jungle, plains, and poles show native plant and animal life. Tabs and flaps take you deeper into the action by unveiling hidden animals.

The Human Body, by Jonathan Miller. Viking, 1983.

This book shows joints, muscles, bones, and blood and demonstrates how they all work together. Pull-tabs uncover the parts and indicate the life-support processes of the human body. You'll enjoy sharing this with an adult (one reads, one pulls).

The Mighty Giants, by Stewart Cowley. Warner, 1988.

Dinosaurs seem to leap off the page in this book, which resembles a pop-up birthday card. They are believably real when portrayed in the water. A group of four or five dinosaurs is shown foraging on each of four double pages, with each dinosaur identified by name. The long caption serves as a text and relates the animals on the two pages to one another, providing information on their size and habits.

Strange Animals of the Sea. National Geographic Society, 1987.

Each double page of the book opens with a three-dimensional scene from the sea. Flaps and pull-tabs let you investigate the world hidden by rocks and plants. The goosefish opens his wide mouth, and his green eyes stare right at you; next, another fish swims through a hole in the coral.

Your Amazing Senses. Aladdin, 1987.

The five senses are demonstrated using touch and color tests, scratch 'n' sniff, and coordination and reflex checks. The relationship of the senses to the brain is emphasized. Sometimes you can fool your brain.

I Want a Book about Kids Who Want to Write

Charlotte the Starlet, by Barbara Ware Holmes. Harper, 1988.

Her mother thinks Charlotte should turn her imagination (lies) into a novel, but Charlotte doesn't think she looks like a writer. Pippi, her cat, doesn't seem to care what Charlotte does; in fact, Charlotte can't come up with a single idea and is so disgusted and angry that she throws peas at dinner. Aha! Why not write her anger into a book? She writes and becomes popular at school, but other things worry her—like real friendships and really good writing.

Dear Mr. Henshaw, by Beverly Cleary. Morrow, 1983.

Leigh Botts writes letters to Mr. Henshaw, his favorite author; to Mr. Pretend Henshaw (a fictional author for Leigh's diary, suggested by Mr. Henshaw himself); and to ~~Dear Mr. Henshaw~~ when he realizes that he wants to write what *he* (not what Mr. Henshaw) thinks. He uses his ability to write as a focus for his not-too-great life after his parent's divorce.

Harriet the Spy, by Louise Fitzhugh. Harper, 1964.

Harriet watches the people who surround her and writes about them in her notebooks because she wants to be a writer. Ole Golly, her nurse, tells her it is good training. When the notebooks are discovered, however, she loses what few friends she has—even her best friends; and Ole Golly isn't there anymore, although she has written Harriet her advice—apologize and lie a little. Harriet discovers that it takes courage to go back to school and is surprised when she is named editor of the Sixth-Grade Page. She nearly blows it—again.

Hey World, Here I Am! by Jean Little. Harper, 1986.

Emily and Kate are friends; and Kate writes mostly poetry, sometimes putting Emily in her poems. With some prose interspersed, the poems are about people, school, the outdoors, and other things. They contain well-chosen words and phrases that give a vivid picture of the world around them.

Julia and the Hand of God, by Eleanor Cameron. Dutton, 1977.

In the California of the 1920s, a thoughtful girl first begins to realize her ambition to be a writer. On her eleventh birthday her Uncle Hugh gives her a book with blank pages, hand-lettered *The Private Journal of Julia Redfern;* and Julia knows she will enjoy recording in it what's happening to her.

Mysteriously Yours, Maggie Marmelstein, by Marjorie Weinman Sharmat. Harper, 1982.

The student who wins the competition to write the Mystery Person column in the school newspaper must be a good writer—and a good keeper of secrets. The column must be short, not obscene or libelous—and increase the paper's popularity. Maggie wins the competition and soon realizes the whole school wants to be in the Mystery Person column. Maggie's job soon goes to her head, but a fan letter and a counterfeit column convince her she should pass on the power to someone else.

The War with Grandpa, by Robert Kimmel Smith. Delacorte, 1984.

Peter admits he will miss slipping into his dad's office to write the story (for his teacher) of the time when his grandpa came to live with them. He and his grandpa have moments of real war and others that are more like war games, but they never lose sight of the logic and joy of the peaceful settlement concerning whether Peter's room in the house is best for grandpa to have.

Write On, Rosie! by Sheila Greenwald. Little, 1988.

Rosie decides to become an investigative reporter; it coincides with her need for an LLA (lifelong ambition). She pays attention in the writing workshop and chooses an interesting person to interview—the headmistress of her school. Then she gets it all wrong. She meant to write the truth—not fiction. Rosie decides she is best able to write about how she *lost* her LLA.

I Want a Book about Ghosts or Ghosts and Kids

America's Very Own Ghosts, by Daniel Cohen. Dodd, 1985.

You don't have to look in spooky castles or in strange, faraway places. Lincoln, Houdini, and Edison all have ghosts of themselves wandering around right here in America. Edison even tried to invent a machine to talk to the dead! The nine stories in this collection will make even the strongest doubter start to wonder if ghosts really exist.

Christina's Ghost, by Betty Ren Wright. Scholastic, 1985.

Tomboyish Christina is not thrilled at the prospect of spending the summer with her stuffy Uncle Ralph, but she is excited about uncovering the mysteries at the musty old house in Wisconsin. Her excitement turns to fear, however, when she encounters a ghost in the attic. She is very glad when her uncle understands they must escape, and they become friends.

The Ghost of Windy Hill, by Clyde Robert Bulla. Crowell, 1968.

Professor Carver agrees to take his wife and their children, Lorna and Jamie, to live at Windy Hill for one month, just to discover if there is a ghost there. The family discovers a lovely home; Bruno, a beggar boy; and a strange woman, Miss Miggie, who wears a long white dress and a flowery hat. Although there are mysterious happenings, they fail to find a ghost; and when their month is up and the owner is due back, they reluctantly prepare to leave. A surprise ending gives a good account of the legendary ghost and promises new and happier events.

The Ghost Squad Breaks Through, by E. W. Hildick. Dutton, 1984.

Four ghosts use a computer to communicate with two living boys, and together they form the ghost squad. On Case Number One, Wacko breaks a boy of his habit of stealing and accusing others of it. The next case, however, is to prevent a jewelry store robbery; and Wacko and Buzz go to the police with reliable information from the ghosts—Danny, Joe, Karen, and Carlos.

The Ghost Upstairs, by Lila Sprague McGinnis. Hastings, 1982.

When his house is torn down, twelve-year-old Otis White moves in with Albert, the boy next door. The trouble is—Otis is a ghost! Albert shows Otis all kinds of things that have been invented in the seventy-five years since he was killed, and Otis can't resist trying them out. Erratic behavior of the bicycle ensues, for example; and Otis must look for another home—possibly the new public library that will have a computer!

The Haunting of Grade Three, by Grace Maccarone. Scholastic, 1987.

The psychic investigation (the ghost) committee of Mr. Jenkins's class is one of five; and on it are Norma and Debbie, the brains; Adam, not afraid of ghosts; *big* Chuck; Dan, who is under the impression he is a misfit; and Joey, who is usually off in another world. Blackwell House, an old mansion rumored to be haunted, is being used for all the third-grade classes in Elmwood. The committee members separately secure information from the library, the historical society, interviews, and on-site inspections. They decide they need to see the old house at night! They wind up in a storm sewer, where the school custodian finds them. When the transportation committee reports that the river is tidal, the ghost committee realizes that the water coming in under the house is causing it to shift and create noises. They don't find any ghosts, but the result is a good report, which the communication committee can use in the town's newspaper.

The Secret in the Sand Castle, by Laura Lee Hope. Pocket Books, 1988.

The Bobbsey twins are back and on vacation in Beachcliff Bay. Why does a mirror break when no one is around; why do Bert and Freddie get locked in the cellar? Flossie finds a hidden door, but Nan says it's just the back staircase. Then they find out about the treasure. Where is it? And why have ghosts appeared from time to time?

Spooky Thanksgiving, by R. A. Montgomery. Bantam, 1988.

Pretend that your family has moved to a big, scary old house in Plymouth, Massachusetts. Open a door and out comes a giant turkey from which you must get away—by choosing one of several different solutions.

T. J.'s Ghost, by Shirley Climo. Crowell, 1989.

On a foggy California beach, T. J. meets a boy who tells her he sailed from Australia on the *Coya*. When she learns that the *Coya* sank offshore more than a hundred years ago, she realizes the boy must be a ghost. He teaches her some rhymed slang and tells her about his life. She locates his gold ring and goes to the beach expecting to see him. A wave knocks her out, and afterwards she finds tricks and pranks written in the sand. Does that tell you the rest of the story?

Wait Till Helen Comes, a Ghost Story, by Mary Downing Hahn. Clarion, 1986.

This is a scary story! Molly is to look after her new younger stepsister Heather, and she knows Heather is strongly influenced by the discovery of a tombstone in the old graveyard near their parents' studio-home in a country church. It is strange that the initials and the ages on it are the same as Heather's. Heather has bad dreams and talks to Helen, her friend—a ghost; and Molly has to drag her from the lake to save her from Helen.

Who Knew There'd Be Ghosts? by Bill Brittain. Harper, 1985.

Tommy and his friends love to play around the deserted old Parnell house, but they learn that a stranger, Mr. Katkus, plans to buy it and tear it down. They don't want to lose their playground! With help from the two resident ghosts, they save the old mansion and discover the secret Mr. Katkus was searching for.

The World's Most Famous Ghosts, by Daniel Cohen. Dodd, 1978.

You've probably heard that Lincoln's ghost has been seen in the White House. There are descriptions in this book of other famous people's ghostly appearances in London, New Orleans, West Point, and at sea, to mention a few. Some of the stories have been seriously considered. After you read, decide what you want about ghostly legends.

Do You Have Any Books about Indians?

Buffalo Hunt, by Russell Freedman. Holiday, 1988.

The buffalo meant survival to the Plains Indians. The hunt was dangerous, and every member of the tribe (even children) helped prepare the meat and skin of the animals for useful purposes after the hunt.

Death of the Iron Horse, by Paul Goble. Bradbury, 1987.

Sweet Medicine, a Cheyenne prophet, foretells the coming of the white people and the destruction to follow. Years later, in 1867, in an effort to defend their people from a terrifying creation of the white people called the Iron Horse, Cheyenne warriors cut through the ties and pull up the rail bed spikes with tomahawks and knives. When they succeed in derailing a Union Pacific freight train, the Indians enjoy its contents and then burn it, wiping out their fears.

The Goat in the Rug, as told to Charles L. Blood and Martin Link by Geraldine. Parents, 1976.

Geraldine, a very ticklish goat, explains how mohair (her wool) becomes a traditional Navajo rug woven by her friend Glenmae. Geraldine is cautious at times; a pest at times; and, as the rug in the loom increases in size, very companionable and almost possessive of the rug, because there is a lot of her wool in it.

Jenny of the Tetons, by Kristiana Gregory. Harcourt, 1989.

Carrie has no love for Indians; they recently killed her parents and kidnapped her brothers; but a fifteen-year-old girl living in Idaho Territory in 1875 has few choices. Beaver Dick needs someone to help his wife with the children, and Carrie is astonished to learn that his wife Jenny is a Shoshone Indian. Carrie's plans to escape are repeatedly postponed as she grows to understand and appreciate Jenny and Beaver Dick's relationship; Miles, the young carpenter from the fort; and the land around them.

The Sign of the Beaver, by Elizabeth George Speare. Houghton, 1983.
When the first steps of homesteading are complete, Matt is left to tend the garden, care for the cabin, and hunt for his own food while his father goes to get the rest of the family. Matt's future looks bleak until a chance meeting with an Indian and his grandson provides him with an opportunity to learn the ways of the people of the beaver, who teach him hunting skills that enable him to survive until his family arrives.

Sing Down the Moon, by Scott O'Dell. Houghton, 1970.
The promise of the spring of 1864 comes to an abrupt end when the Long Knives (white soldiers) capture the Navaho Indians of Canyon de Chelly and force them to march to Fort Sumner. Many suffer from exposure to the weather, hunger, illness, and fear. Bright Morning is one of the few able to keep their dream of returning to their beautiful homeland.

Sweetgrass, by Jan Hudson. Philomel, 1989.
Sometimes Sweetgrass gets so angry! Her parents don't think she is mature enough to get married, and she is now the oldest not-yet-married girl in her Blackfoot Indian tribe. She works hard butchering buffalo and tanning hides, but no one ever notices. She wishes she were more like her grandmother, She-Fought-Them Woman, the great warrior. What will she have to do to prove herself? Her opportunity comes when she saves her family from a smallpox epidemic.

Where the Buffaloes Begin, by Olaf Baker. Warne, 1981.
Little Wolf often dreams of the buffalo. In the spring of his tenth year, he creeps from his tepee and rides southward to where the buffalo herd begins. After many hours of watching—and after remembering the song of Nawa, the wise man, and the legend told by his ancestors of the buffalo arising mystically from the middle of a secret lake—Little Wolf sees them and shouts in response to the spectacle. The noise arouses the herd, which surrounds him and his horse; but the buffalo do not seem to intend to harm him, and he begins to enjoy the ride. Then he sees that the direction taken by the herd will cut off a surprise Assiniboin raid on his own people.

I Need a Tall Tale

The Diane Goode Book of American Folk Tales and Songs, collected by
  Ann Durell. Dutton, 1989.

  A slice of Americana awaits you in this collection of stories,
music, and songs. You can meet Yankee Doodle, Davy Crockett,
and the Knee-High Man. You can sing "I've Been Working on the
Railroad," dance to "Buffalo Gals," or read "The Greedy Wife,"
a tale from Puerto Rico.

John Henry: An American Legend, [retold] by Ezra Jack Keats. Pantheon, 1965.

  John Henry, a black American railroad worker, was born with
a hammer in his hand. At least that's the way the folktale starts. As
a young man he leaves the riverboats and joins the railroad builders.
A new steam drill can do the work of six men in cutting a tunnel
through the mountains, and John Henry takes the challenge with
a hammer in each hand.

John Tabor's Ride, by Edward C. Day. Knopf, 1989.

  John Tabor is a complainer. As a young whaler, he goes away
on his first long voyage and complains to his shipmates about the
food, the work, the weather, and the long time at sea. One night, an
odd little man spirits him away on a frightening worldwide voyage—
aboard a whale! Grateful to return to his ship after the horrendous
journey, John is forever cured of his complaining, and sailors like
to be on a ship with this jolly whaler.

Johnny Appleseed, a Tall Tale, retold by Steven Kellogg. Morrow, 1988.

In real life, he is John Chapman, born in 1774 in Massachusetts. He becomes the legendary Johnny Appleseed when he leaves home, clears a plot of land, and plants apple seeds from the pouch he carries. He continues doing this across the country, going as far as Indiana. The settlers who come, as he thought they would, want to buy his trees. Sometimes he gives his trees away. One legend tells how he is able to get the land cleared for his largest orchard in a contest with a gang of woodsmen!

The Narrow Escapes of Davy Crockett, by Ariane Dewey. Greenwillow, 1990.

Davy Crockett has many narrow escapes. According to the title page of the book, he escapes from a bear, a boa constrictor, a hoop snake, an elk, an owl, eagles, rattlesnakes, wildcats, trees, tornadoes, a sinking ship, and Niagara Falls! Davy has considerable strength, but what do you think he uses for transport going *up* the falls?

Paul Bunyan Swings His Axe, by Dell J. McCormick. Caxton, 1936.

Paul, the legendary lumberman of the North Woods, grows to enormous proportions early on; a cradle the size of a ship is anchored off the coast of Maine to rock him to sleep. You may not know that spilled ketchup accounts for the Red River Valley or that Paul Bunyon helps his friends dig the St. Lawrence River—the outcome being rather curious, as the settling of a bet also results in the Thousand Islands sort of being invented.

Pecos Bill and Lightning, by Leigh Peck. Houghton, 1968.

Here are the rip-roarin' stories cowboys tell about their hero. Pecos Bill is plenty tough and plenty brave; and he travels the Southwest, inventing things such as the lariat, barbed wire, and tumbleweeds! He lets the weather alone but falls in love.

Whoppers, Tall Tales and Other Lies, collected by Alvin Schwartz. Lippincott, 1975.

One hundred and forty-five exactly, and Schwartz claims to know more in the introduction—more lies, that is, and not ordinary but fun ones. *Whoppers* also contains a lot of one-liners, which are vital to brief tall tales and apt to be ones you haven't heard *yet,* can remember easily, and will find useful in conversation.

Where Are the Animal Books?

ANIMALS

Faithful Elephants: A True Story of Animals, People and War, by Yukio Tsuchiya. Houghton, 1988.

The Japanese army fears the consequences if Tokyo's zoo is bombed directly and the dangerous animals escape. The zookeepers are ordered to kill the animals, including the favored three performing elephants. Only an immediate end of the war will save the elephants' lives and relieve a zookeeper's sorrow.

Gray Boy, by Jim Arnosky. Lothrop, 1988.

Gray Boy is Ian's dog, and their relationship is very special to Ian since his father's death. For Gray Boy the year of puppyhood is soon over, and he is roaming farther and farther from home as a full-grown, mixed-breed Newfoundland. His hunting instinct leads him to a neighbor's rabbit hutches—and the need to escape punishment afterward. It is several months before Ian hears about a severely wounded dog and goes to him with his rifle—for what purpose, he is not sure.

Harvey's Marvelous Monkey Mystery, by Eth Clifford. Houghton, 1987.

Nora, Harvey Willson's cousin, is visiting them, as she usually does every summer, and she's just as peculiar as ever. However, when a monkey appears, Harvey and Nora share in the experience, lopsidedly but sufficiently to have a lot of fun together. Their parents, the neighbor Mrs. Motley, and the police are in on the capture of the animal-napper. They find that Aloha is a special monkey trained to help a handicapped person and that he belongs to Zena Worth, who lives in a nearby town.

Mr. Popper's Penguins, by Richard and Florence Atwater. Little, 1938.

The first penguin, Captain Cook, is a gift to Mr. Popper, whose enthusiasm for explorers and explorations has triggered its surprise arrival. Next, Greta is sent from an aquarium because both penguins seem to be sick—probably from loneliness. The Poppers cannot really afford them; the penguins need ice and fresh fish in large quantities. When the penquin family, twelve of them by now, start their play, the Poppers notice their games and decide that the stage is the place for them and a way to make money for their upkeep. Despite the penguins' success, Mr. Popper still has an important decision to make. Will the next stop be Hollywood or the North Pole?

The Story about Ping, by Marjorie Flack and Kurt Wiese. Viking, 1933.

Ping is a Chinese duck who lives on a houseboat in the Yangtze River. When he dawdles on his way back to the houseboat, he is caught and put under a basket all day. The boy who catches Ping turns him loose before his mother can cook him, but Ping is still late getting home—and is punished.

Warton and the Contest, by Russell E. Erickson. Lothrop, 1986.

Two toads, Warton and Grandpa Arbuckle, and a field mouse named Neville set out to retrieve Grandpa Arbuckle's watch-compass, which a crow has stolen. Unfortunately, when they reach the crows' headquarters, they are caught and put to work polishing all the bright objects the many crows have collected. Warton manages to escape, and, with the help of Bike, a blind crow, is able to rescue Grandpa Arbuckle and recover the watch-compass.

The Wild Christmas Reindeer, by Jan Brett. Putnam, 1990.

After nearly a year on the tundra, the reindeer are reluctant to return to Santa's winter farm. Teeka is in charge of training Bramble, Heather, Windswept, Lichen, Snowball, Crag, Twilight, and Tundra for the Christmas run. The grooming goes rather well, but the harnessing upsets them; the next day they can't seem to pull together. When their antlers lock, Teeka yells too much; the antlers won't budge, and it's nearly Christmas Eve. Teeka cries, tells the reindeer she's sorry, and promises not to boss them. As the team relaxes, the antlers jiggle free. Next day they look great as they practice turning right and left, and Santa takes off on time.

Zucchini, by Barbara Dana. Harper, 1982.

Zucchini, a black-footed ferret of the weasel family, is a member of an endangered species; but he is more immediately endangered by his curiosity, as he wonders whether there is a world outside his cage in the Bronx Zoo. On his way to Oklahoma, he finds that there *is* a world—one with lots of people in it. He also has the persistent feeling that he must decide about Billy, who is ten and very shy and who doesn't speak up for Zucchini, although he understands and loves him. He leaves the prairies and returns to the American Society for the Prevention of Cruelty to Animals, where he finds Billy again.

BEARS

Andy Bear, a Polar Cub Grows Up at the Zoo, by Ginny Johnston and Judy Cutchins. Morrow, 1985.

When Andy Bear is born on Christmas in the Atlanta zoo, he is no larger than a guinea pig. His parents are two Siberian polar bears who have been together in the zoo nearly twenty years. Constance Noble, one of the keepers, rescues Andy and takes him home in order to feed him every hour and a half. Andy dislikes noise, opens his eyes after four weeks, cuts his baby teeth, and, after another five weeks, walks. When he weighs twenty-five pounds, he is returned to the zoo clinic, where he is lonesome for Constance. At five months, and still a baby, he weighs fifty-five pounds and is moved to an outside zoo cage. He easily learns to like ice and ice cream and grows to adulthood, weighing one thousand pounds and standing eight feet tall.

Beady Bear, by Don Freeman. Viking, 1954.

Beady, a toy bear, discovers bears are supposed to live in caves, and he leaves his house to find one. He walks up and down the hill, fetching a pillow, newspapers, and a flashlight to feel more at home. When Thayer comes looking for his toy bear, he has the wind-up key that Beady needs; and he wants Beady to come home. They find that they need each other!

Gentleman Bear, by William Pene Du Bois. Farrar, 1985.

Bayard goes to boarding school, the 1936 Olympics, and World War II—and gets kidnapped the day Queen Elizabeth is crowned. He takes his human Sir Billy Browne-Browne with him, of course.

Bayard's name was chosen by Billy from a long list, which was suggested by Billy's father and read aloud by Billy's mother. It means "a gentleman of courage and honor," which Bayard certainly is. He is also Billy's best friend since 1920 *and* his economic support in 1985, because Bayard is one of the most famous teddy bears in the world.

Happy Birthday, Moon, by Frank Asch. Prentice-Hall, 1982.
It would be nice to give the moon a birthday present. Bear crosses the river, goes through the forest, and climbs a mountain to be close enough to the moon to be heard. When Bear talks to the moon, he finds out that the moon's birthday is the same day as his and also that the moon wants a hat. Bear sets out to buy a fancy dress hat. It is all *very* logical.

The Teddy Bear Tree, by Barbara Dillon. Morrow, 1982.
A magic tree in Bertine's backyard blossoms with teddy bears. She discovers that all these bears need lots of attention; and if they do not get enough, they can be very ornery. She had been reluctant to part with even one since they arrived, but now she is having a party for her friends—a find-a-new-home-for-a-bear party.

We're Going on a Bear Hunt, retold by Michael Rosen. McElderry, 1989.
One brave dad, four brave children, and a dog swish the grass, splash the river, and squelch the mud, going on a bear hunt on a beautiful day. They are not scared by any obstacles until they reach a gloomy cave. Inside the cave, there's a bear! It is back over everything for everyone until they are home under the covers!

CATS

The Broccoli Tapes, by Jan Slepian. Philomel, 1988.
While in Hawaii for five months, Sara sends cassette tapes to her teacher in Boston as part of her oral history project. She and her brother Sam find a very wild cat on the beach, which they feed and love, naming it Broccoli. They meet and become friends with Eddie Nutt, too. Moments of happiness and sadness make the time fly— something they had not expected.

Cat Tales, by Sara Pitzer. August House, 1989.
As you read in this book about various cats, which seem very

familiar to you, you'll wonder if the author interviewed some of the cats you know! Think about what a cat's name means to it and its owner, and also read the author's definition of why a cat has nine lives!

Cat Walk, by Mary Stolz. Harper, 1983.

Barn cats do not have names and stay away from humans, but the black one with white feet becomes the pet of Missy, who calls him Tootsy-Wootsy. He moves from one name to another for various reasons. Later he arrives at an animal shelter, where he makes friends with a mouse, a parrot, and other animals but eventually gets a home and another name. He misses his animal friends, however, and starts back to them and the name he had at the shelter, Max.

The Fur Person, by May Sarton. Norton, 1957.

A kitten leaves his birthplace when he is six months old and is adopted by two housekeepers. They know how to treat a cat-about-town and name him Tom Jones. They love him, protect him, and nurse him; he gives a bit more of his real cat-self to them than usual but still takes rambles outside until he feels the tug of home—and humans. That is when he becomes a fur person.

Jenny and the Cat Club, by Esther Averill. Harper, 1973.

Gentle Jenny Linsky, the captain's cat with the red scarf, watches the cats gather at the foot of the tree in her backyard. The other cats ask her to join, but she is scared that there will be nothing that she can do as well as they. When she receives ice skates, they see her skate and ask her again to join. It is the beginning of many activities for Jenny because she is voted into the club.

One-Eyed Cat, by Paula Fox. Bradbury, 1984.

Ned refers to it as the time when he was scared and worried about telling a lie. Feeding a cat, which may be the one he had shot at, and knowing that it survives the winter are not as important as telling the people who knew or suspected his actions—old Mr. Scully and Mama.

Uncle Whiskers, by Philip Brown. Little, 1974.

Born in 1959, this kitten's most outstanding characteristic is its richly marked ginger fur, but Uncle Whiskers is truly special. When he recovers the next year from an accident that leaves him with the use of only his two hind legs, he masters astonishing feats of strength, retains his joy of life, and lives until 1972.

CATS AND KITTENS

Cats' Eyes, by Anthony Taber. Dutton, 1978.

As a kitten, Tiger looks you directly in the eye. Better still is Tiger's view of everything as he grows up. The pencil-sketch drawings often include Tiger. They resemble the ones in a family's memory book—but these pictures are done from the viewpoint of the cat.

Cross-country Cat, by Mary Calhoun. Morrow, 1979.

It is a good thing that Henry the cat is a hind-leg walker. He uses this skill when he's accidentally left behind at the family's mountain cabin. The snow is deep, and there is no food, so he straps on some homemade skis, which the children had tried on him once, and sets off cross-country toward town.

The Cricket in Times Square, by George Selden. Ariel, 1960.

Chester Cricket eats money, and the mouse Tucker likes to save it; Harry Cat shows them how to manage it—and not let Mario's parents lose any at their newsstand in the New York City subway. Chester sounds like a harp when he chirps, and he chirps when he doesn't feel too good—which accidentally starts him on a musical career. More than seven hundred people are late to work the first day because they stop to listen to him.

The Dancing Cats of Applesap, by Janet Taylor Lisle. Bradbury, 1984.

One girl and one hundred cats bring a moment of fame to Applesap, New York, and it's going to appear in *The Guinness Book of World Records.* Melba Morris, aged ten, is perhaps the shiest person in the world; she prefers Jiggs' Drug Store to the Super Queen, where the rest of the kids hang out. At the drugstore, Miss Toonie takes care of the cats while the owner plays sad guitar music; neither of *them* is going to do anything about the lack of business, so it's up to Melba to turn it around.

The Diary of a Church Mouse, by Graham Oakley. Atheneum, 1987.

It is surprising, but Sampson the cat is a good friend to the church mice. He is not so much of a friend that he shares his saucer of milk, but he is an okay friend otherwise, according to Humphrey the mouse, who is writing his autobiography. Unfortunately for them, Sampson brings home a beautiful cat whose favorite food is mice. They manage with ingenuity to scare the monster away, and Sampson returns two days later—for his milk, presumably.

Martin's Mice, by Dick King-Smith. Crown, 1989.

Even from his kitten days, Martin doesn't want to catch mice to eat; he wants them as pets. This seems more reasonable to him, however, than it does to the mice. Martin enjoys Drusilla and her eight young mice for a few days; but after that, families of cats *and* mice with many ''maydays'' keep him far too busy. Also, when Martin is bought and made into a pet, *he* doesn't like it!

Moses the Kitten, by James Herriot. St. Martins, 1984.

The name Moses comes easily to a black kitten, which is rescued by a vet from the rushes by the pond. The Butlers have plenty of cats on the farm, but they decide to keep the kitten and put him in the warmest place in the barn. Moses likes the milk of the mother pig, who is feeding a new litter of piglets! It is strange sight, but it works.

Puddums, the Cathcarts' Orange Cat, by Nancy Winslow Parker. Atheneum, 1980.

When Puddums, normally quiet, starts acting really crazy, his owners are worried. Even the vet doesn't seem to know why the cat is acting so wild. It takes the girl next door to find the solution to Puddums's mysterious behavior. And you'll never guess until you read what it is.

Rotten Ralph, by Jack Gantos. Houghton, 1976.

How can any one cat be so horrible? Ralph is Sarah's cat, and he enjoys wrecking parties and making fun of people. Will he ever learn his lesson? Sure he will. Sarah's family leaves him at the circus that he has disrupted, and he has to work! When he finally manages to escape to the real world—the world of alley cats—that, too, proves uncomfortable. Will he ever be loved again?

Socks, by Beverly Cleary. Morrow, 1973.

The Brickers are a young couple, and they want the kitten with the white feet—Socks. His fine feline life is disrupted when a baby is added to their home; then Nana, who is critical of Socks, visits. He is put outside and must now be contented with looking in the window to satisfy his curiosity. As Charles William grows older, Socks becomes an inside cat again; but it takes some time for the Brickers, Charles William, and Socks to agree on what that means.

DRAGONS

A Book of Dragons, by Hosie and Leonard Baskin. Knopf, 1985.

Saint George is probably the most famous of all dragon fighters, and he fought a fire-breathing monster. The many other very fierce and famous dragons from mythology and literature described in this book include a coward, a fold-up dragon; a beautifully bejeweled dragon that is on a page in a manuscript; and a very small and powerful dragon that resembles a rooster.

Dragon of the Lost Sea, by Laurence Yep. Harper, 1982.

Civet, a cruel and wicked witch, steals and magically imprisons the Inland Sea within a pebble. The dragon princess Shimmer tries to rid herself of the human boy Thorn, but she is won over by his offer to help her. With the odds against them, the two new friends go into battle against Civet.

Eddie's Blue-Winged Dragon, by C. S. Adler. Putnam, 1988.

Handicapped with cerebral palsy and held back unfairly by the prejudice of others, Eddie takes solace from his best friend, Gary, his sister, Mina, and his new glass and brass dragon. At times the dragon seems to come alive. Can it really be seeking revenge on those who treat Eddie unfairly? How was the fire on the hill started? Eddie learns about controlling anger by possessing the dragon and about his disability when he participates in an essay contest.

Everyone Knows What a Dragon Looks Like, by Jay Williams. Four Winds, 1976.

An imminent attack by the wild horsemen threatens the citizens of Wu. The poor boy Han doesn't know whether to believe that the little old fat man who arrives just before the attack is truly a dragon who can save them. No one else believes it's true. Han's politeness and courtesy are appreciated, and the dragon sets his power against the city's enemy and saves them all.

The Flight of Dragons, by Peter Dickinson. Harper, 1979.

Although the text is difficult, you will enjoy the numerous illustrations while learning more about dragons. The author's theory that dragons are, for the most part, not legendary but real is based on their specialization—flight. Their flights required large body size, the ability to breathe fire, and a particular chemical reaction in their bodily fluids. This amazing idea is backed up by excerpts from various literary sources.

The Reluctant Dragon, by Kenneth Grahame. Holiday, 1938.

A peaceful, and possibly cowardly, dragon is befriended by Boy. When St. George arrives to slay the dragon, Boy explains to him that his friend is good and a gentleman besides! The three meet secretly and agree to *stage* a fight for the villagers so that the dragon will also be invited to the banquet afterward.

Saint George and the Dragon, adapted by Margaret Hodges. Little, 1984.

A fierce dragon has been laying waste Princess Una's kingdom. The young and inexperienced George, a Red Cross Knight who was raised by the Queen of the Fairies, accompanies Una back to her homeland to rid it of the dragon. The battle of knight versus dragon lasts three days. George wins Una for his bride and goes on to become the famous Saint George, the patron saint of England.

Sarah and the Dragon, by Bruce Coville. Lippincott, 1984.

Grabbed by a dragon, Sarah is whisked to his castle. She sends her pocket companion, Mrs. Bunjy, a ladybug, to get help from her grumpy unicorn friend Oakhorn. He and Sarah's Aunt Mag set out to the rescue. Once freed from a spell, Toad the dragon is a lonesome little man, whom Sarah learns to like. They all take part in Sarah's return home.

Weird Henry Berg, by Sarah Sargent. Crown, 1980.

Henry feels closer to animals than he does to humans sometimes, and he considers Vincent, a lizard, a perfect pet although a bit weird. Henry discovers he must hide him from Professor Ferguson; from Aelf, a creature with teeth like an alligator's who flies at night; and from Millie, an elderly woman who believes Vincent is a baby dragon. When Henry learns who Vincent really is, he agrees that Millie must take Vincent from Oshkosh, Wisconsin, to Wales.

PIGS, PIGS, PIGS

Babe, the Gallant Pig, by Dick King-Smith. Crown, 1983.

Won by Farmer Hogget, Babe is adopted by Fly, the farm's dog, and taught, along with four puppies, to be more like a dog than a pig. Babe's politeness is appreciated by the sheep she herds and saves—from thieves and a pack of dogs. But she scores her biggest victory when she wins the Grand Challenge Sheep Dog Trials as a sheep pig.

Mrs. Pig's Bulk Buy, by Mary Rayner. Atheneum, 1981.

Ten piglets love tomato ketchup and put it on everything their mother cooks! When the supermarket has a sale on ketchup, Mrs. Pig decides to give them their tummies' desire: tomato ketchup served at *every* meal, including breakfast. The piglets aren't sure they like cornflakes and ketchup. If you ate tomato ketchup at every meal, would you turn piglet pink, too?

Nothing But a Pig, by Brock Cole. Doubleday, 1981.

The pig Preston has pretensions to better things; and although his owner Avril considers him his best friend, Preston readily sees himself as a gentleman's pig. When the landlord, Mr. Grabble, comes to collect the year's rent, he demands the pig as payment, takes him, and installs him in a pen. Preston decides to spruce himself up. He goes into the house, has a snack, takes a bath, and dresses in Mr. Grabble's fine suit. He is naturally mistaken for Mr. Grabble's visiting uncle! Should Preston continue in his new role or go home?

Pig Pig Grows Up, by David McPhail. Dutton, 1980.

Pig Pig is the last of the children to grow up—if he ever will. His mother is exasperated, discouraged, and unable to handle the stroller with Pig Pig and the groceries in it. It rolls dangerously down the hill but Pig Pig instinctively does the right thing and doesn't act like a baby.

Piggins, by Jane Yolen. Harcourt, 1987.

The Reynards are giving a dinner party. The guests arrive; and Piggins, the proper butler, announces, "Dinner is served." Suddenly the lights go out, and Mrs. Reynard's diamond lavaliere is stolen! Did the butler do it? In classic detective style Piggins tells them how it happened, the thieves are discovered, and the lavaliere is recovered.

Tales of Amanda Pig, by Jean Van Leeuwen. Dial, 1983.

Amanda Pig confronts the breakfast egg she really doesn't want to eat, makes an imaginary airplane trip in the living room, scares the monster clock in the hall with the help of her father, and has a spat with her brother Oliver. Finally, when it's time for bed, Amanda and her mother switch places, with Amanda performing all the bedtime rituals until Mom falls asleep!

The True Story of the 3 Little Pigs, by A. Wolf as told to Jon Scieszka. Viking, 1989.

Alexander T. Wolf (also known as the Big Bad Wolf) tells his side of the story: He was framed by the news reporters. What's more, the first little pig wasn't very smart, the second little pig was only a little smarter, and the third little pig made a rude remark about the wolf's granny. Now you'll have to decide which story is the true one!

The Witch's Pig, a Cornish Folktale, retold by Mary Calhoun. Morrow, 1977.

A pig is the object of a dispute between Betty Trenoweth, who people believe is a witch, and her cousin Tom, who is certain he can outwit her. Although the pig behaves as if it is bewitched (it won't fatten, for instance), Tom still thinks he has the power to tame it. Does he?

UNICORNS

Learning about Unicorns, by Laura Alden. Children's Pr., 1985.

You will learn something of the history of the mythical unicorn and how best to find one, as well as discover the magical powers within a unicorn's horn. The Barnum and Bailey Circus once claimed to have four unicorns, but the claim was disputed. Stories about them continue.

Michael Hague's World of Unicorns, by Michael Hague. Holt, 1986.

The mysterious unicorn with its slender horn appears in the center of fairyland in this pop-up book. He exerts his magical powers to heal and to leap into the air yet remains modest. In the unicorn's presence, the creatures of fairyland do not feel threatened.

Sarah's Unicorn, by Bruce and Katherine Coville. Lippincott, 1979.

Sarah lives with her Aunt Mag, who, once kind and lovable, has turned into a witch. One day, after noticing that a cut of Sarah's heals quickly—almost magically, she decides to follow Sarah to find the source of her healing power. When she discovers Sarah's friend, the unicorn Oakhorn, she attempts to capture him. All the other animals, especially a ladybug, help Sarah to save Oakhorn. Oakhorn breaks the spell that is on Sarah's Aunt Mag, and she becomes lovable once more.

The Tale of the Unicorn, by Otfried Preussler. Dial, 1989.

Hans goes unarmed with his two older brothers to hunt a unicorn. On the journey, one brother marries, and the other finds gold. Hans takes their weapons and goes on, meeting an old man whose advice he follows to find the unicorn. He starts to shoot but cannot pull the trigger to kill such a beautiful creature.

The Unicorn and the Lake, by Marianna Mayer. Dial, 1982.

When a drought threatens the lives of the animals, a noble unicorn from a faraway mountain uses his magical horn to make it rain. The unicorn also overwhelms an evil serpent, purifies the water, and then leaves the animals to live in harmony again.

Unicorn Crossing, by Nancy Luenn. Atheneum, 1987.

Jenny believes in unicorns. The sign by the driveway says Unicorn Crossing, and she feels certain that this must be the right place to see one, for there are trees, quietness, and the faint scent of cinnamon. She meets Mrs. Donovan, who owns their summer vacation cottage; and they pick rose petals, place them in the birdbath, and wait.

Unicorn Moon, by Gale Cooper. Dutton, 1984.

In her dreams, a princess goes to the land of Unicorn Moon seeking a young man riding a horse that has one silver horn. He tells her that the answer to a riddle will break the spell cast upon him. When she awakens, she searches throughout the kingdom to find the meaning of true love. Through her actions, she brings the young man to life, and they define true love for us.

The Unicorn Treasury, compiled and edited by Bruce Coville. Doubleday, 1988.

Everyone knows what a unicorn is. Well, yes—and no, says
Coville. He provides a basic description of unicorns in the introduction, in which he admits no one knows for certain if they existed
or where—leaving us with a tantalizing mystery. Seventeen other
famous authors provide stories, poems, and excerpts about the unicorn.

I Like Trick Books

Bet You Can! Science Possibilities to Fool You, by Vicki Cobb and Kathy
    Darling. Avon, 1983.

Can you put a pencil through a plastic bag full of water and
not spill a drop? Can you outpull four big people in a tug-of-war?
These and sixty other tricks seem impossible, but all of them are
based on scientific principles that are easy to understand. Each one
is described with the preliminary step that you must do, and then
the result of that action is explained and illustrated.

Black and White, by David Macaulay. Houghton, 1990.

You are warned to inspect everything that follows the title
page in this book. In the upper fourth of the first double-page spread
is an illustrated story entitled "A Waiting Game," which involves
newspapers. Why not start reading and looking there? In addition,
three other stories begin in the same way and tell about a burglar,
a family of four with a dog, and train transportation. In a book—
especially if it's a good one— you usually have to wait until the end
to see what happens. This book keeps its promise of making you
wait to the end.

Cat's Cradle, Owl's Eyes: A Book of String Games, by Camilla Gryski.
    Morrow, 1984.

This book teaches you how to prepare string for games and
storytelling and presents illustrated instructions for figures from
around the world. In addition to the popular cat's cradle and its
variations, there are figures and stories to trick your friends. In
"Cutting the Hand," your friend's wrist is caught in a tangle of

strings, and then, with a pull of your thumbs, it's free. "The Yam Thief" escapes with sacks of yams, seemingly knotted on your fingers; and just try to catch "The Fly."

Chancy and the Grand Rascal, by Sid Fleischman. Little, 1966.

Soon after the death of their father in the Civil War, their mother dies; and the Dundee brothers and sisters are separated. Chancy, the oldest, sets out to find the others. Along the way he meets his Uncle Will, the grand rascal in the family. Together, while rafting down the Ohio River, they outwit the unscrupulous Colonel Plugg and then rescue Chancy's sister Indiana in Paducah, Kentucky. The three of them walk to Sun Dance, Kansas, where the other two children are, a town where they all just might stay together as one family.

The Contests at Cowlick, by Richard Kennedy. Little, 1975.

Hogbone had hoped to stir up a little trouble in Cowlick and is glad that Wally, a little kid and the only one in sight, offers him four very funny contests: footracing, climbing, horselifting, and hollering. Wally manages to eliminate Hogbone's gang, and only Hogbone is left to compete in hollering.

Danny, the Champion of the World, by Roald Dahl. Knopf, 1975.

When Danny discovers his father's love of poaching pheasants, he worries, because he knows that the nasty landowner, Mr. Victor Hazell, will stop at nothing to catch Danny's father. When Mr. Hazell plans his annual snobbish opening-day shooting party, Danny thinks of a plan to ruin it; and his father names it Sleeping Beauty. Their actions net them more than one hundred birds, but what do you do with that many birds, whether they belong to you or someone else?

The Hateful Plateful Trick, by Scott Corbett. Little, 1971.

When their baseball game is canceled due to rain, Kerby and Fenton are very bored, so they really don't mind earning a little money by baby-sitting with Kerby's little cousin Gay. Then they start experimenting with a chemistry set given to them by a strange old woman, Mrs. Graymalkin. To their horror, they find that each one smells like the food he or she hates the most. Their efforts to get rid of the smells lead them on a series of adventures, and only with the help of Mrs. Graymalkin can they reverse the trick.

The Stories Julian Tells, by Ann Cameron. Pantheon, 1981.

Julian, who is seven, loves to tell stories—usually big whoppers—about some of his ordinary, everyday situations. He convinces his younger brother Huey that cats come from a catalog and help plant gardens; he charges his classmates one cent each to see his "cave-boy teeth"; and he tries to grow faster by eating fig leaves.

263 Brain Busters: Just How Smart Are You, Anyway?, by Louis Phillips. Viking, 1985.

The answers are in the back—which permits you to use your brain and think before you look—that is, check to see if you know the right answer. A few are considered easy on the brain, so you can be comfortable with this book.

Unriddling: All Sorts of Riddles to Puzzle Your Guessery, collected by Alvin Schwartz. Lippincott, 1983.

Trying to solve these riddles from American folklore should "strengthen the brain," if you believe as people in the past did. The book has several kinds of riddles that are not used today, such as leg riddles, but all of them can be used now for fun.

Do You Have Any Books like Shel Silverstein's?

Dirty Dinky and Other Creatures, by Theodore Roethke. Doubleday, 1973.

The slightest uncomfortable feeling is called Dirty Dinky, and you and he are part of each other. Most of the other creatures in the poems are animals—whale, yak, lizard, rat, donkey, and heron, to name a few—but the animals do not have names; except for turtle, who is called Myrtle.

Ghastlies, Goops and Pincushions: Nonsense Verse, by X. J. Kennedy. McElderry, 1989.

Half of the collection is ghastlies; then come some limericks with some goops and hardly any pincushions. There are lots of rhymes, a variety of subjects, and lots of fun.

The Hopeful Trout and Other Limericks, by John Ciardi. Houghton, 1989.

If you are a limerick fan, you will love this collection, featuring characters, events, animals, and situations—most of which are very funny but with a few that are kind of sad or thoughtful.

I'm Mad at You, selected by William Cole. Collins, 1978.

Whenever you're mad, whether it's just a little bit or a lot, you'll be able to find a poem in this collection about how you feel. You will find a poem to fit a situation, such as "Bickering," and a type of person, such as "Cry-baby"; and perhaps after sampling a few of them, you will not be a "Crosspatch" yourself.

The New Kid on the Block, by Jack Prelutsky. Greenwillow, 1984.

The first poem is about a kid, whom you might recognize, in a new neighborhood. All the rest of the poems are about people, who may or may not live on any block you know, or about creatures, such as an alley cat with one life left.

Nonstop Nonsense, by Margaret Mahy. Macmillan, 1989.

If you appreciate the silly and the strange, you will enjoy this collection. In fact, if you like nonsense, you will be pleased that these stories and poems are just the right length and use details, flourishes, and refrains to build really funny situations.

Poems of A. Nonny Mouse, selected by Jack Prelutsky. Knopf, 1989.

The talented poet, A. Nonny Mouse, will finally get credit for all those nonsense poems mistakenly attributed to anonymous poets, because Prelutsky takes up her cause. In an exchange of letters that is still going on, they agree that four of Prelutsky's poems will be included in the book of over seventy-two rhymes, with A. Nonny Mouse's name properly spelled in the title.

I Want a Gross Book

Body Noises, by Susan Kovacs Buxbaum and Rita Golden Gelman. Knopf, 1983.

Do you ever wonder why your body sometimes makes embarrassing noises—and what to do if some of those things happen when you're with others? Although the book gives the reasons, you may still have to say "excuse me."

Horrible Harry and the Green Slime, by Suzy Kline. Viking, 1989.

Harry really isn't all that horrible, but sometimes he *does* have some wild ideas. He suggests celebrating the end of the teacher's reading of *Charlotte's Web* by putting cobwebs all over the school. A recipe for his green slime, in case you need it, is included.

How to Eat Fried Worms, by Thomas Rockwell. Watts, 1973.

Could *you* eat one worm a day for fifteen days? Billy's friends bet him that he can't do it. There are a few rules about which worms are allowed (not those on tomatoes), but the worms are provided by Billy's friends; there also must be witnesses to the eating. How far will Billy go to win his bet?

How to Haunt a House for Halloween, by Robert Friedhoffer with Harriet Brown. Watts, 1988.

You don't have to wait until October to start grossing out your friends with these disgusting disguises and tricks, such as piercing an arm, slashing yourself with a knife, and making a real bloody mess of swatting a fly.

Mummies in Fact and Fiction, by Arnold Madison. Watts, 1980.

Mummies have been preserved throughout history. Included in this account are photographs and facts about shrunken heads, bog mummies, and modern mummies. In movies, television, books, and plays, mummies are not numerous; the same ones remain popular over the years. Cryogenics is the scientific name for mummification as it is currently practiced.

The Slimy Book, by Babette Cole. Random, 1986.

Short but definitely *not* sweet, this story is about the different kinds of slimy things that are all around us, like slime in drains and food, and possibly slimy things from Mars—in a dream.

Slugs, by David Greenberg. Little, 1983.

Whatever you do to a slug, watch out! If you swallow a slug, perhaps chocolate-flavored or with your spaghetti, be careful, because, as these verses go on to detail, slugs might do equally vile and unsavory things to you to get their revenge.

Those Amazing Leeches, by Cheryl M. Halton. Dillon, 1989.

From a colored photograph showing leeches attached to an infected toe to information on how to keep and observe leeches, this book has everything you ever wanted to know about them—the majority as bloodsucking parasites and *more!* The history, mystery, and scientific use of leeches are discussed in an informative way.

Why Does My Nose Run? (And Other Questions Kids Ask about Their Bodies), by Joanne Settel and Nancy Baggett. Atheneum, 1985.

If you've ever wondered what makes people sneeze, yawn, throw up, burp, or itch, this is the book for you. Find out the scientific reasons behind fifty-one things that your body does.

Do You Have Any Books
on How to Save the Earth?

Desert of Ice, Life and Work in Antarctica, by W. John Hackwell.
  Scribner, 1991.

Antarctica has an early history of exploitation by human out-
siders, but in 1958 it became an experiment in demilitarization and
scientific cooperation. Conservation is also an aim of the twelve
nations that are responsible for research in Antarctica. Expeditions
are usually for sponsored research, but some personal trekking is
allowed. A member of an Australian research team in 1989, Hackwell describes the extensive preparations needed to conduct such
an expedition, as well as transportation facilities, life on a base, and
several interesting studies, including one on the emperor penguins.
The future uses of Antarctica's resources are debated, and one issue
is whether it would be best just to leave it alone, since that way it
may be more valuable to the world.

Endangered Species, by Sunni Bloyd. Lucent, 1989.

Throughout the world, many animals and plants are disappearing, as people destroy their habitats or hunt them to extinction.
Some, like the passenger pigeon, are gone forever. Others, like the
buffalo, black-footed ferret, and whooping crane, seem to be safe,
while the fates of the tiger, rhinoceros, and condor are still in doubt.
Many people are making an effort to save these species and to protect the rain forests; and there are things that you can do to help.

Every Living Thing, by Cynthia Rylant. Bradbury, 1985.

You will soon discover the link that connects one animal to the
next and one person to the next. The variety of people is as interest-

ing as the twelve animals are appealing, and they are especially appealing when they come in contact with the people.

I Am Leaper, by Annabel Johnson. Scholastic, 1990.

Having the gift of tongues, Leaper, a kangaroo rat, decides to speak to the scientists about the monster that is destroying the desert. They are amazed, recheck their instruments, but never listen to her message. Leaper also communicates by thought with Julian, who feeds and waters the animals in the laboratory. He saves her from a dangerous trip back to the desert by taking her on his motorbike and thinks he has lost his best friend because she considers him part of the machine that she calls the monster. He learns something about the tough life that animals must endure and knows that a responsible person can do something to preserve natural surroundings.

Just a Dream, by Chris Van Allsburg. Houghton, 1990.

Walter travels into the future, but it isn't like the one on television that promises a personal robot and all the doughnuts he wants. It is threatening and illogical—no more than a bad dream, he hopes—but he knows that it may happen. When he is home again safely, he starts to make the world he saw in his dream—his own real world—a better place; and he follows his friend Rosie's idea of planting a tree for the future on his birthday.

I Wonder If I'll See a Whale, by Frances Ward Weller. Philomel, 1991.

Before today, the whales have always been in the distance. Now, she is watching especially hard to see a whale. Perhaps it will be Midnight, Appaloosa, or Trunk—names the sailors have given them. Suddenly, Stormy, her friend, says the spout ahead belongs to a humpback, and the boat's engine is stopped. The whale dives, and they wait for another look or for another whale. Then, friendly Trunk (so called because of a stunted fin) breaches—not just once. He looks right at her. In a single glance they are friends.

I Want a Skinny Book

ABOUT SOMEBODY FAMOUS,
NOT REAL LONG . . .

Hulk Hogan: All-Star Wrestling, by Don Ward. Creative Education, 1986.

Hulk Hogan's trademarks are his theme song "Eye of the Tiger," his mane of white-blond hair, and his huge six-foot-seven size. What you might not know about the Hulkster is that he got his start in the movie *Rocky III;* that he's originally from Florida; and that some people aren't sure, despite his being a world champion, if he's a great wrestler!

Homesick, My Own Story, by Jean Fritz. Putnam, 1982.

Jean Fritz is an author who writes about history, and this book is her own history. She lived in China sixty-five years ago with her parents, who were missionaries. She writes of what she ate, where she went to school, and how it felt to grow up so far from America.

I'm Nobody! Who Are You? The Story of Emily Dickinson, by Edna Barth. Seabury, 1971.

A quiet and shy young woman used her poetry to show others her inner strength and zest for living. She liked being like a child; she liked being alone; she liked to write her thoughts in letters and poems. More and more, she wrote poems that she put in the bottom drawer of her dresser. Her sister Lavinia and a friend of Emily Dickinson, Mabel Todd, selected 115 poems for publication four years after her death in 1886. Other books of her writings appeared, and she became a major American poet.

Jim Henson, Muppet Master, by Nathan Aaseng. Lerner, 1988.

Did you know that the famous Kermit the Frog was made from Henson's mother's old green overcoat? Jim Henson was fascinated by television, and his own puppets helped him to get his start. When ''Sesame Street'' started in 1969, his Muppets became known to everyone, but they nearly ruined his career!

Meet Edgar Degas, by Anne Newlands and the National Gallery of Canada. Kids Can Pr., 1988.

Edgar Degas, a French painter who lived more than 150 years ago, tells us about his pictures. He selected scenes from the ballet and horse racing to show the way bodies looked in motion. He tells us what or whom he is painting, how he composed the scene, and why he was interested in doing each particular piece of art illustrated in this book.

Picasso, by Mike Venezia. Children's Pr., 1988.

Many people believe that Pablo Picasso is one of the great twentieth-century artists. Picasso varied his work greatly from year to year: at times his figures look realistic and at other times nonrepresentational in a style that is called *abstract.* Picasso's paintings, reproduced in this book in color, provide us with an excellent understanding of his life and artistic periods.

Pocahontas, by Carol Greene. Children's Pr., 1988.

Born about 1596, Pocahontas was the daughter of Chief Powhatan. Captain John Smith taught her English, and she saved his life more than once and called him brother. Pocahontas was one of the first Indians to live in England, where she went to show the English people what Indians were like. She died there in 1617.

Shaka, King of the Zulus, by Diane Stanley and Peter Vennema. Morrow, 1988.

Shaka was just a little boy when he and his mother Nandi were driven from a Zulu clan because Shaka's mother objected when his father punished him. The children laughed at Shaka, but his mother told him he would be a famous chief one day. Later, he did become the leader of all the Zulus and trained a band of fierce and skilled warriors. To the Zulus of today, Shaka is a hero, his reputation lasting although he has been dead for over a hundred years.

Who Said There's No Man on the Moon, by Robert Quackenbush. Prentice-Hall, 1985.

Jules Verne was a Frenchman who wanted to travel from the time he was a small boy. As a writer he learned to travel by way of his lively imagination. In his books he took people around the world on a hot-air balloon trip, to the bottom of the sea in a submarine, and—in the 1850s—to the moon. People loved his adventure stories, and he became very rich indeed; but he never stopped dreaming of new adventures.

GOOD, SHORT NEWBERY BOOKS

Call It Courage, by Armstrong Sperry. Macmillan, 1940.

The villagers ignore him, and the great chief refuses to call him son, so Mafatu, a young Polynesian boy, sets out to conquer what he fears most—the sea. He reaches a sacred island in his canoe and faces all the dangers there. Having proved his bravery to himself, he makes a very difficult journey home and hears his father tell the villagers that his son's name is *Mafatu,* "Stout Heart."

Dear Mr. Henshaw, by Beverly Cleary. Morrow, 1983.

Leigh Botts writes letters to his favorite author, Boyd Henshaw, in second, third, fourth, and fifth grade because he really likes his book *Ways to Amuse a Dog.* In sixth grade he has to do an author report, and the answer he gets from Mr. Henshaw upsets him; but the correspondence continues and changes his life in a surprising way.

From the Mixed-up Files of Mrs. Basil E. Frankweiler, by E. L. Konigsburg. Atheneum, 1967.

Claudia works out a brilliant runaway plan: she and her brother Jamie will live in the Metropolitan Museum of Art in New York City! It doesn't solve her personal problems; but a beautiful marble statue, possibly the work of Michelangelo, intrigues them sufficiently for them to pursue its origins. Claudia understands more about art, secrets, and runaways after a visit to Mrs. Frankweiler.

A Gathering of Days, by Joan W. Blos. Scribner, 1979.

Catherine Cabot Hall, aged thirteen, begins her journal on October 17, 1830, and records her school, church, and household life on a small New England farm where she lives with her father and sister. She closes her journal on March 8, 1832, after her father remarries and just as she is about to go to Aunt Lucy to help her with her new baby.

Number the Stars, by Lois Lowry. Houghton, 1989.
The year is 1943, and the place is Denmark. Annemarie Johansen and Ellen Rosen, who is Jewish, are best friends. When the German troops begin to round up all the Jews, Annemarie and Ellen pretend to be sisters. Then, late one night, Nazi soldiers come to the Johansen house and question why Ellen is not blond like her sister.

Sarah, Plain and Tall, by Patricia MacLachlan. Harper, 1985.
Caleb and Anna anxiously await the arrival of Sarah, the plain and tall woman who answers their father's ad for a new wife and mother. Now that she is here, she will give it a try for one month before deciding between returning to her home near the sea or remaining on the farm in the middle of the prairie. The children hope she will stay and be part of the family.

Sounder, by William H. Armstrong. Harper, 1969.
Wounded by a sheriff's posse, Sounder, the devoted coon dog, waits for his beloved master's return from jail. No longer a hunter or very spirited, Sounder can barely manage to meet his master's son when he returns for the summer field work. However, Sounder's rich voice signals the return of his owner, whose withered body prevents any work or hunting—except for one last time. Sounder returns alone to the house to get the boy.

The Whipping Boy, by Sid Fleischman. Greenwillow, 1986.
The heir to the throne had never been spanked in his life! An orphan named Jemmy serves as the whipping boy for Prince Brat. Jemmy dreams of running away and so does the prince. As it happens, the two set out, get caught by outlaws, escape, and go home, *both* to be punished by the king!

SHORT ONES

Fifth Grade: Here Comes Trouble, by Colleen O'Shaughnessy McKenna. Scholastic, 1989.
Collette can't figure out why her friend Marsha wants to celebrate her eleventh birthday with boys at her party. *Friends* are

supposed to come to parties; all the boys Collette knows would trip you for fun. Marsha's cousin Carole is thirteen and plans to guide Marsha into her teen years early, but her ideas nearly get the three of them in jail for shoplifting and almost cause a cancellation of the party at Skateland.

The Great Gerbil Roundup, by Stephen Manes. Harcourt, 1988.
It is an okay place, an ordinary small town, until INTERPETCO buys the gerbil farm. Their first effort, establishing a unique museum, is a success. In an effort to keep the town of Gerbil, Pennsylvania, on the map, Elton Wazoo, whose father is the company's manager, and his friend McBeth McBeth, an imaginative girl in Elton's class, stage a gerbil roundup on the Fourth of July.

Justin and the Best Biscuits in the World, by Mildred Pitts Walter. Lothrop, 1986.
He is a mere ten years old and the only male in his family, so Justin has a difficult time fitting into a household of women. His grandfather, who is alone and lives on a ranch, teaches him to appreciate a number of things Justin has overlooked about cooking and housekeeping.

Robin Hill, by Carol Greene. Harper, 1986.
Robin Hill does not like Mr. Potts, the family's landlord; and she draws him as a monster in her picture of an imaginary enchanted forest. It is a decision too quickly made, because he is the one who rescues her when she falls.

Stories about Rosie, by Cynthia Voigt. Atheneum, 1986.
Rosie is black and white and furry with bright eyes. She tells us about her life inside and outside the house and about the family that takes care of her and imposes a few rules, such as when to bark. From a dog's perspective, that is almost as interesting as when Rosie meets a deer while everyone is picking blueberries.

A Tale of Middle Length, by Mary Francis Shura. Atheneum, 1966.
The thing (a mousetrap) among the mice brings them to a realization that worth is not based on their places of origin or the length of their tails. Alec is an older field mouse and knows that Dominie, a house mouse, has not quite told him the whole truth about her life; but it is Dominie who recognizes the danger of the thing. Both go to heroic extremes to save Mortimer, who likes to play on the seesaw in the middle of the thing; and Alec is proud of

the young mice who are clever enough to use the thing as a catapult to finish off their enemies.

Vinegar Pancakes and Vanishing Cream, by Bonnie Pryor. Morrow, 1987.

Life is a constant struggle for Martin Elwood Snodgrass. All the others in his family are famous, competitive, and busy—even Robbie, who is two years old. Martin's red hair makes him an unmistakable member of the family, but being the shortest kid in third grade and having a name like Martin Elwood Snodgrass are drawbacks. A garden, a kitten, tenting—and Robbie—are hard to beat for bringing out the best in a family.

SHORT, THIN, ABOUT ANYTHING

April Fool, by Mary Blount Christian. Macmillan, 1981.

Seth the Dreamer, whom everyone considers worthless, volunteers to try to save the village in which King John may build a house, totally disrupting the people's usual life. They can think only of leaving or fighting, but Seth sets up many funny incidents, which lead the king to believe that they are *all* fools. Was this the first April Fools' Day?

Dracula Is a Pain in the Neck, by Elizabeth Levy. Harper, 1983.

Has Dracula ever visited you in camp? Does he really exist? Robert's older brother Sam courageously initiates Operation Garlic and stops the howling and ''bat'' joking. Robert and Sam find the kitchen raiders wearing capes and fangs, but Robert's Dracula doll *seems* to be smiling. Why?

Patrick and the Fairy Thief, by Margaret Wetterer. Atheneum, 1980.

Are fairies really crafty Little People who put a spell on people and make them dance forever? Certainly Patrick's mother disappeared a year ago, and Patrick has to hang on tightly to his brown cow, which his mother gave him and which answers to his special whistle, as the music and dance whirl around them. He doesn't realize it is a trial of three that will break the spell cast on his mother.

The Problem with Pulcifer, by Florence Parry Heide. Lippincott, 1982.

Pulcifer's problem is that he can't seem to enjoy watching television! Everyone—his parents, his teacher, the remedial television teacher, even a psychiatrist—tries to help him, but all Pulcifer wants to do is to read books. What will come of a boy who only wants to read when everyone else watches television all day?

The Teddy Bear Tree, by Barbara Dillon. Morrow, 1982.

The next-door neighbor is not ready to believe the first ten bears that Bertine picks from a bear tree—bears that walk and talk. Bertine names one Joel, and he talks to humans. He suggests to her that three bears are enough and expects her to resolve the problems ten bears have caused.

The Wonderful Mrs. Trumbly, by Sally Wittman. Harper, 1982.

Some say Martin is in love with his teacher; others call him teacher's pet. Martin hopes he and Mrs. Trumbly are really best friends. He watches her romance with the music teacher, Mr. Klein, develop with some alarm, but relaxes a little when she thanks him for his presents. When he has a new teacher in the fall, yes, he and Mrs. Klein remain friends.

SKINNY

An Actor's Life for Me! by Lillian Gish as told to Selma G. Lanes. Viking, 1987.

A famous actress, Gish was born in 1896 in Springfield, Ohio, and was on stage when she was almost six and on Broadway when she was ten. She went to California for her health and to be with her family—and became a star in silent movies.

Alvin Webster's Surefire Plan for Success (and How It Failed), by Sheila Greenwald. Little, 1987.

When Alvin learns that there's going to be a new baby in his family, he concocts an elaborate plan to show that he's still the best. First, he'll learn about sharing because he is paired with Bone, who needs help with his math and has twin baby sisters, whom Alvin likes. He thinks he succeeds as the best tutor when Bone gets a perfect grade on the math exam. He is totally upset when his own score is sixty!

Buffalo Hunt, by Russell Freedman. Holiday, 1988.

The buffalo were plentiful and the biggest animal on the plains, standing six feet high at the shoulder and weighing a ton or more.

The hunt and the work of preparing each part of the slain buffalo for the tribe's use played a vital part in the Indians' lives. The coming of the white people in the early 1800s changed that way of life, and herds of buffalo were destroyed.

The Canada Geese Quilt, by Natalie Kinsey-Warnock. Dutton, 1989.

When her grandmother decides to make a quilt for the new baby and asks Ariel to design it, Ariel draws the geese flying north; but the geese are flying south before Ariel sees her family's life return to normal following her grandmother's slow recovery from a stroke. They finish the quilt in time for the baby's arrival, and Ariel is suprised when she recieves one, too. Perhaps you can guess part of the design.

Germy Blew It, by Rebecca C. Jones. Dutton, 1987.

Jeremy Bluett wants to appear on television and comes up with a number of clever schemes, including a school strike and a bubble-gum-blowing contest, all of which end in hilarious disasters—and in a financial loss of $10.55, which he must repay.

Justin and the Best Biscuits in the World, by Mildred Pitts Walter. Lothrop, 1986.

A week on Grandpa's ranch teaches Justin a lot of things, including the fact that housework and cooking are not necessarily done only by women. At a festival, Grandpa wins a blue ribbon for his biscuits, and Justin's basketball skills in the bean-bag contest win him a first prize. Before he leaves, Justin asks his grandfather how he makes biscuits!

Rats! by Pat Hutchins. Greenwillow, 1989.

Sam saves enough money, at last. Now the problem is to talk his mother and father into letting him actually buy a pet rat. Both Sam and his brother James agree that Mom has to be won over first. It works, but curiously they never do figure out how they managed to convince their mother. Soon, Nibbles the rat comes home in a cage that their father chooses!

Shaka, King of the Zulus, by Diane Stanley and Peter Vennema. Morrow, 1988.

Shaka, the great African military leader, was born in 1787, the son of a chief when the Zulus were not important or powerful; but he became a respected warrior who used new methods of fighting. After he became chief, he trained his soldiers to march fifty miles a day—something foot soldiers had never been able to do. He ruled little more than ten years and was assassinated, but his life story is still told with pride.

Stringbean's Trip to the Shining Sea, by Vera B. Williams and Jennifer Williams. Greenwillow, 1988.

A series of funny postcards and a number of pictures trace the adventures of Stringbean and his older brother, as they travel by truck to the Pacific Ocean and give us an original and funny look at America.

Volcano: The Eruption and Healing of Mount St. Helens, by Patricia Lauber. Bradbury, 1986.

This is a chronicle of the mountain that awakes in 1980, flattening forests, causing lava flows, and destroying plants and animals. The story also covers the survivors and colonizers who make a comeback. Life on Mount St. Helens is again possible.

THIN CLASSIC

All-of-a-kind Family, by Sydney Taylor. Follett, 1951.

Ella, Henny, Sarah, Charlotte, and Gertie live with their parents in New York City. In 1912–1913 the day-to-day life of this warm Jewish family includes visiting the public library on Fridays; dusting with the hope of finding a penny; going to the pushcart market; celebrating the Sabbath; and being sick, stubborn, or surprised—all with one to five girls involved.

Ben and Me, a New and Astonishing Life of Benjamin Franklin as Written by His Good Mouse Amos, lately discovered, edited, and illustrated by Robert Lawson. Little, 1939.

The *true* life of Benjamin Franklin is told by Amos the mouse, who finally reveals all the secrets that contributed to Franklin's successes. Amos recollects his participation in them and is neither particularly awed by Franklin nor is he left out since Amos is often in Ben's fur cap. The result is a humorous account!

The Borrowers, by Mary Norton. Harcourt, 1953.

Members of the miniature-sized Clock family, known as the Borrowers, live under the floors of a large English house, completely hidden from the view of the human beings who legally live there. An unfriendly housekeeper begins to suspect that something strange is going on, and Arrietty Clock is seen by *and* talks to a human boy. Will any harm come of this?

Charlotte's Web, by E. B. White. Harper, 1952.

The magic of love takes place on a farm where a little girl named Fern has a pig named Wilbur who makes friends with a spider, Charlotte, and a rat, Templeton. Wilbur especially sees to it that Charlotte's 514 unborn children survive the winter after Charlotte dies.

The Fourth of July Story, by Alice Dalgliesh. Scribner, 1956.

After the representatives of the thirteen English colonies agreed to declare their independence from England, they selected a committee of five to set forth their beliefs and asked Thomas Jefferson to do the writing. After the signing of the Declaration of Independence on July 4, 1776, in the Philadelphia State House, the document was read before many groups around the country, and the date of Independence Day became our most important holiday.

The Great Brain, by John D. Fitzgerald. Dial, 1967.

Tom, who is fair but smarter than anybody else, is The Great Brain of Adenville, Utah, in 1896, according to his brother. He outwits friends and relatives and always manages to make a profit for himself! Tom sells ninety cents worth of junk (marbles, a slingshot, etc.) to Basil, the Greek immigrant boy, when he realizes that Mr. Kokovinis desperately wants his son to have a friend, learn English, and play games. Tom's brother is not surprised when Tom agrees to Mr. Kokovinis's offer to give Tom anything he wants; he hopes Tom doesn't envision taking over the restaurant in the deal. He is capable of it.

Half Magic, by Edward Eager. Harcourt, 1954.

Summer vacation looms ahead, threatening to be as boring as ever for Jane, Mark, Katharine, and Martha—until Jane finds a coin that magically brings adventures that take them all over the world. They are a bit slow to realize that it provides only half what they wish for when they get a desert—but not the island—on the first wish.

I Want a Book Where Disasters Happen

Amazing Escapes, by Thomas G. Gunning. Dodd, 1984.

These nine true stories are hard to believe. They are bizarre, yet they really happened to real people. The majority of the escapes happen in this century, in the air or sea. Two families are involved in one escape with their children. All are "lucky, courageous, or daring," the author says in the introduction, because they wanted "to stay alive and live free."

The Chernobyl Catastrophe, by Graham Rickard. Bookwright, 1989.

The managers of the Forsmark nuclear power station in Sweden check their own facility for radiation leakage on April 28, 1986, when the detector registers one hundred microrems an hour, compared to the usual four. Now we know the radiation came from the Chernobyl nuclear power station in the Soviet Union, where a quarter of a million schoolchildren under the age of ten had to be evacuated from the vicinity of the explosion. Above all, Chernobyl shows that most countries are not prepared for such an emergency.

Downwind, by Louise Moeri. Dutton, 1984.

Although he is the oldest of four children, twelve-year-old Ephraim feels he's in the middle. His parents expect him to communicate with them and to spend a lot of time taking care of Jocelyn, a whiner; Bones, who is bigger and heavier than Ephraim, even though he is younger; and sometimes Caleb, the toddler. These responsibilities are almost too much for Ephraim when the news reports a meltdown at a nuclear power plant, and the family joins hundreds of others on the highway to get out before the radiation is spread downwind to their area. When the danger is past, Ephraim reflects on what happens in a near-disaster situation and the meaning of responsible action.

High Tide for Labrador, by Eve Bunting. Childrens Pr., 1975.

Jimmy hates the man who is in love with his widowed mother, even though it is Big Jim who is responsible for getting him a job aboard his cod-fishing boat, which is bound for Labrador. The routine trip turns into a perilous nightmare when the ship heads directly for an iceberg. Thirteen-year-old Jimmy struggles not only against the icy seas but also against his changing feelings for Big Jim, as he tries to find within himself the meaning of courage and maturity.

Medicine Walk, by Ardath Mayhar. Atheneum, 1985.

Burr and his father are on their way to Albuquerque, and Burr feels sure his cousins will be there to celebrate his twelfth birthday. His father agrees this time to fly over the Petrified Forest. When Burr's father has a heart attack and crash-lands before he dies, the deviation in plans means no one is apt to find the small Cessna airplane. Grief-stricken, afraid, and alone, Burr realizes that if he is to survive, he must leave his father's body with the plane, take what food and water are available, and start out across the desert. The teachings of the Apache foreman on the family's ranch prove invaluable as he struggles to survive.

Night of the Twisters, by Ivy Ruckman. Crowell, 1984.

Dan and Arthur are on their bikes and sense the change in the wind, but Arthur is sleeping over, so they go back to Dan's house for the usual evening of television—until the severe-weather announcement comes on. While his mother goes to check on an elderly neighbor, Dan and Arthur take Dan's baby brother Ryan to the basement. They can hear the roaring of the tornado as it tears the house above them and their neighborhood apart. They wonder if anyone, including their families, can possibly have survived.

I Need to Do
a Science Project

How to Do a Science Fair Project, by Salvatore Tocci. Watts, 1986.

Everything you'll need to know can be found in these nine chapters: choosing a topic, types of projects, planning, doing an experiment, the scientific method, preparing a report, analyzing data, exhibiting, and presenting the project to the judges.

Ideas for Science Projects, by Robert Gardner. Watts, 1986.

Over one hundred ideas range from easy to more advanced. The major topics are: water, astronomy, light, chemistry, physics, heat, electricity, and the human, plant, and animal sciences. Read the introductory discussion about getting into a science project and be alert to the boldface type to be safe.

Magic Mud and Other Great Experiments, by Gordon Penrose. Simon and Schuster, 1987.

Dr. Zed is right in the picture, with statements and questions about each of the twenty-one experiments. Children or animals or both also appear on the pages to help him. In the same place on the facing page you will find a list of things you'll need and a brief description of the scientific action to be examined in the experiment. The steps to make a wind wheel or a boomerang, for example, are numbered, and sometimes a description of how to use these items appears in the text and illustration.

The Marshall Cavendish Library of Science Projects, by Steve Parker. Cavendish, 1986.

Six books on science experiments cover the areas of earth,

light, mechanics, plants, the human body, and water. These books are full of fascinating experiments, projects, and facts and are accompanied by many colorful illustrations and pictures.

My Sister, My Science Report, by Margaret Bechard. Viking, 1990.

Phoenix Guber, the least desirable person in the class, is selected by their teacher to be Tess's partner on a science report. Since she doesn't like barn owls, Tess agrees with Phoenix that her older sister Jane, ''an adolescent in its natural habitat,'' is okay as a subject for research. Jane objects, of course; but Phoenix and Tess get to know each other so much better during the work on their project that when Tess wins four front-row seats to the Ice Extravaganza, she has to decide whether she will ask Phoenix.

Science Fair: Developing a Successful and Fun Project, by Maxine Haren Iritz. Tab, 1987.

This is a clear, detailed guide on how to complete a successful science project. It takes you from choosing a topic to the judging of it and helpful pictures of completed projects are included. There are appendixes with ISEF (International Science and Engineering Fair) project categories, summaries of projects, and award winners' abstracts. ''Sugar substances which ants prefer'' is an easy project; many are harder.

Where Are the Books with People and Things Hiding in the Pictures?

Anno's Animals, by Mitsumasa Anno. Collins, 1979.

Be assured that there are many animals hidden in the trunks, branches, and leaves of countless trees and in the undergrowth. You will moan and groan over the lack of a more exact key for these challenging illustrations.

Demi's Find the Animal A•B•C, an Alphabet-game Book, by Demi. Grosset, 1985.

You may spend hours looking for the perfect match, comparing each of twenty-six animals with others of the same kind among the many possibilities in each double-paged, colorful illustration. Thank goodness there is a key. The animals range from large to small; are wild, domestic, or imaginary; and include a number of birds and some fish.

The Eleventh Hour, a Curious Mystery, by Graeme Base. Abrams, 1988.

Elephants are good cooks, so Horace prepares eleven kinds of food for his party. After the eleven guests play eleven games and frolic at his eleventh birthday party, they discover that a theft has occurred. You are expected to look closely at the animals in the pictures, find the one you think is the thief, and decode a message in the back of the book. You are saved because a six-page sealed section tells all.

Find the Cat, by Elaine Livermore. Houghton, 1973.

When the cat takes the dog's bone, the dog starts hunting. Can you help him find the cat? He sees the cat, but it runs away *again*. It's lots harder than you think to find that cat!

PIGS from A to Z, by Arthur Geisert. Houghton, 1986.

You are really challenged as you look for seven piglets who are building a tree house in each picture, and as you look for five alphabet letter forms on each page. You must also find the preceding letter and the next letter. You can do it! Check the last three pages for a key to help you.

Where's My Hat? by Neil and Ting Morris. Little, 1982.

With the money she has saved, Emma buys a new straw hat with red ribbons. While she is in the park, it blows off. Can you follow the thief and find Emma's hat plus ten other mystery objects in each picture?

Where's Waldo? by Martin Handford. Little, 1987.

After Waldo introduces himself, you'll spend hours trying to spot him in intricate illustrations as he goes around the world. Each double-page spread contains a postcard message from Waldo. He's catching a train or boarding a plane; he's going to a museum or to the zoo. Use your eyes! You'll find him in the crowds. Waldo is also careless and loses things. Can you find them?

Where's Wallace? by Hilary Knight. Harper, 1964.

Try finding Wallace, a little orange orangutan, who leaves his cage at the zoo to find adventure in other places, like the museum, the beach, and a department store. When his friends cannot find him, they are sad; but he is in his favorite place, and guess where that is?

I Want a Book Where Kids Eat Something Icky

Beetles, Lightly Toasted, by Phyllis Reynolds Naylor. Atheneum, 1987.

In his attempt to win the annual essay contest, Andy submits a collection of unusual recipes, starting with beetle brownies. The contest topic is conservation—the fifth grade is urged to be inventive—and Andy shares first place. The publicity, however, is a different matter: He must offer proof that his recipes work by eating his creations in front of the camera!

The Boy Who Ate Dog Biscuits, by Betsy Sachs. Random, 1989.

More than anything else in the world, Billy Getten wants a dog. In fact, he wants a dog so badly that he snacks on dog biscuits instead of cookies; but he also saves a few biscuits for the dogs at the veterinarian's office, where he helps Dr. Mike exercise the strays. His work there is more satisfying than the antics of Howard, his best friend; or of Sarah, his baby sister; or his birthday, for which his grandparents have come—especially since the latest stray, a little dog with a brown-and-black patch around one eye, seems to like him a lot. He is truly surprised the day before his birthday!

Cry Uncle! by Mary Jane Auch. Holiday, 1987.

Davey's mom serves zucchini at each and every meal—until Uncle Will outwits her. He teaches them a good many things about how a real farm operates, but he also spends a great deal of time remembering the early years of his life with his brother. Forced to move in with his niece's family at the age of seventy-four, he is a hard person for Davey to understand. Davey has trouble sorting out his feelings of pride and embarrassment—*except* for the time Uncle Will gets lost in the woods and needs his help.

How to Eat Fried Worms, by Thomas Rockwell. Watts, 1973.

As part of a bet, Billy agrees to eat fifteen worms, one each day, most of them fried. His mother bakes some with onions and sour cream, and Billy is just two bites away from winning when his father orders him to his room. Billy's friend has to smuggle one worm to him so he can win.

Kevin Corbett Eats Flies, by Patricia Hermes. Harcourt, 1986.

Kevin has built a reputation eating insects for money. Why not eat the classroom's exhausted goldfish next? Bailey, his rival, bets five dollars that Kevin can't chew it. Brant, his best friend, asks permission for Kevin to wrap it first in paper, and Bailey agrees, but only if Kevin opens his mouth so she and everyone else can see that he really chews it. Afterward, Bailey and Kevin get off to a slow friendship because they do have one problem in common.

Tales of a Fourth Grade Nothing, by Judy Blume. Dutton, 1972.

Peter wins Dribble at Jimmy's birthday party, and it is his first pet. Knowing his little brother, he should have guessed what could happen when Fudge sees the turtle for the first time and laughs like crazy. Two-and-a-half-year-old Fudge doesn't chew—he just gulps—and then confesses cheerfully that Dribble is in *his* tummy.

I Want a Funny Story

ABOUT SCHOOL

The Beast in Ms. Rooney's Room, by Patricia Reilly Giff. Delacorte, 1984.

Richard Best feels like a beast, left back in the second grade. His old class has moved to a new grade, but Richard is stuck with the same teacher and with new classmates who are smaller than he is. With the help of the reading teacher, the "Beast" makes the transition to the "Best."

Dinosaurs Are 568, by Jean Rogers. Greenwillow, 1988.

Raymond Wayliss refuses to go to kindergarten and is able to avoid it entirely because of his excellent test scores. The following September, Raymond very reluctantly enters his first-grade class with no intention of staying—until he spots a poster of a Diplodocus.

Elaine, Mary Lewis, and the Frogs, by Heidi Chang. Crown, 1988.

Elaine Chow tries to adjust from her life in San Francisco to her new home in Cedarville, Iowa. She and Mary Lewis are assigned to make a flying object for their third-grade science-class project; and they combine Mary Lewis's obsession with frogs and Elaine's asset—a father who will help them make a kite. The final step is to decide what the meaning of a frog kite will be.

I Was a Second Grade Werewolf, by Daniel Pinkwater. Dutton, 1983.

One morning, Lawrence Talbot wakes up hairy—he has become a werewolf! He snarls at his sister at breakfast, makes good speed on all fours part of the way to school, and bites Loretta in class. What fun is being a werewolf, though, if no one seems to notice?

The Magic Book, by Willo Davis Roberts. Atheneum, 1986.
   Enticed by a page on which appears "Spell to put an end to a bully's way," Alex buys an old magic book. He is determined to cast a spell on Norm, the school bully, but the book has a mind of its own; the spell doesn't reappear until several other spells are tried and (sort of) succeed. When it once again appears, Alex and his friends nervously try it out.

Romeo and Juliet Together (and ALIVE!) AT LAST, by Avi. Orchard, 1987.
   When Ed learns that his best friend Pete is in love with Anabell, he and other classmates devise a plan to get them together: They will present an after-school student production of the play *Romeo and Juliet* with Pete and Anabell in the starring roles. Producing the play turns out to be easier said than done, and there is a good deal of audience participation at the performance.

Stage Fright, by Ann Martin. Holiday, 1984.
   Fourth-grader Sara is creative and likes school but is very shy. It is almost the end of the school year, and Sara is looking forward to summer vacation, until her teacher drops the bombshell: The class will present a play at the June festival, and there are enough parts for everyone—including Sara.

Wayside School Is Falling Down, by Louis Sachar. Lothrop, 1989.
   The second book about Mrs. Jewls, her class, and others at the thirty-story high Wayside School consists of thirty short stories, one of which includes a definition of love that so disgusts the dead rat in Mrs. Jewls's desk drawer that it walks away. Wayside School gets a Z+ for zaniness, but it has school situations you will recognize.

Wonder Kid Meets the Evil Lunch Snatcher, by Lois Duncan. Little, 1988.
   The Johnson family moves to a new town in the middle of the school year. On their first day at Summerfield School, Brian and his sister Sarah meet the lunch-snatching gang that picks on anyone who dares to walk through the sixth-grade gate. Lisa and Robbie Chandler share their lunches, and they all discuss how to get rid of a school problem. Brian becomes a caped crusader, and it's Wonder Kid to the rescue.

FUNNY

C.L.U.T.Z. by Marilyn Wilkes. Dial, 1982.

Outmoded robot Clutz, with his bumbling good nature and quirky ways, gets the domestic job that the Pentax family intended for a spiffier, more reliable model. After a string of failures (including a losing score in moonball), Clutz heads sadly to the local recycling plant, where he is found by his best pal, Rodney Pentax. When the family's new robot fails to come through in a very important matter, Clutz comes home.

The Monster's Ring, by Bruce Coville. Pantheon, 1982.

A ring that he bought in a strange magic shop for one dollar comes with instructions in the box; and nice guy Russell Crannacker turns into a hideous monster, capable of scaring the meanness out of the class bully. The third twist of the ring had never been dared—especially on the night of a full moon—and Russell experiences some aftereffects.

The Murder of Hound Dog Bates, by Robbie Branscum. Viking, 1982.

Sass Bates, thirteen, won't rest until he finds and punishes the killer of the pet dog that was his one and only best friend. Funny? Sassafras Bates—Sass, for short—has three aunts who hated the dog; and they are his prime suspects. With Kelly O'Kelly and Clem Watts coming to supper, funny and important things come out in their talking. Sass must further examine the traits of all, even those of his lost dog, when a tornado hits.

The Secret Life of the Underwear Champ, by Betty Miles. Knopf, 1981.

When baseball jock Larry Pryor finds out that he is going to model underwear on television and that all his friends and class-mates will see him, he turns into a nervous wreck. He pretends to his friends that he has to go to New York City to see a dentist, which was how he was first spotted on the street by people from the model agency, who want an athletic eight- or nine-year-old redhead with freckles. After making a second commercial *and* hitting a home run, he can once again enjoy going to the dentist—*honest.*

The Seven ½ Sins of Stacey Kendall, by Nancy J. Hopper. Dutton, 1982.

In order to buy a Bust-ter Sizer, eleven-year-old Stacey decides to earn the money by illegally piercing her classmates' ears and runs into trouble. She finds it hard to write an apologetic essay to present to the school at the awards assembly. Can she? Will she? Will she let her mother edit it?

Valentine Rosy, by Sheila Greenwald. Little, 1984.
Rosy, eager to grow up and in stiff competition with budding sexpot Christi McCurry, is being pushed into having a Valentine party and decides to throw a wicked one. Boys will have to be invited, too, if she and her friends are to avoid being called Babies—as opposed to Belles—in their fifth grade. Little does she know that her party and her rival's party will join her older sisters' party—only to be confined to the kitchen! Rosy wins, of course; the older kids leave after Rosy's friends sing for them.

The Week Mom Unplugged the TVs, by Terry Wolfe Phelan. Four Winds, 1979.
What do three television addicts do when Mom puts the television off limits for one whole, very long week? Their mother's description of them as zombies seems unfair, but their dad supports her plan of action. It so happens that when the week is up, the first program is a rerun—and it is not very exciting compared to the week they have spent with their own version of viewing!

JOKES

The Big Joke Game, by Scott Corbett. Dutton, 1972.
Everyone is mad at Ozzie for making jokes and playing games *all* the time, because sometimes it just isn't appropriate to joke, and his parents are on the verge of sending him to a military school. Ozzie decides to run away from home. He climbs through the window, and just as he is sliding down the trellis, it snaps, and he tumbles to the ground. He wakes up in a land called Limbo that looks like a giant game board and has a guardian devil, Beelzebub. He must solve riddles and make up limericks (and sometimes refrain from these activities) to win the game and get back to earth.

King Henry the Ape, compiled by Charles Keller. Pippin, 1989.
These are short question-and-answer-type jokes, all pertaining to animals; and like the title of the book, they make use of a clever definition or a slight change in the spelling or pronunciation of a word to be funny.

The Joke War, by Gene Inyart Namovicz. Holt, 1987.

John is constantly setting up practical jokes. Charlie, his cousin, finally decides to try a few jokes in retaliation so he can enjoy his summer vacation by the sea with John and the rest of his family. With the help of a neighbor who owns a remote-controlled shark, Charlie devises a practical joke that even John admits is a lulu. The joke that stops the war once and for all is triggered by Charlie's fear that John is in danger on a raft.

The Marigold Monster, by M. C. Delaney. Dutton, 1983.

Nobody likes Audrey's jokes, and nobody will buy marigold seeds from her. Her last chance for a sale, after her mother, is the monster who lives alone in the woods. She ends up telling him jokes. He is slow in catching on, but he has a huge laugh; and enjoys the jokes so much that he agrees to buy $14.32 worth of seeds and wants more jokes. She agrees to tell him more, maybe tomorrow.

Mr. Little, by Robert Newton Peck. Doubleday, 1979.

The new teacher, Mr. Little, is the victim of Drag and Finley, two of his students who love practical jokes. When their most colossal joke on him fails and gets them in trouble, he is not without charity—and advice. They are amazed that he says their jokes are a challenge and that they make his life interesting—but he also tells them to always remember that a practical joke should be fun for everyone.

Treasury of Humor, by Robert Quackenbush. Doubleday, 1990.

This gathering of funny material falls into a pattern according to the months of the year, with each section usually containing poems or a story, a song with music, and some one-liners. There is quite a mix of characters, some of which Quackenbush invented for other books of his but most of whom are animals—all in hilarious situations.

SUPER FUNNY

The Best Christmas Pageant Ever, by Barbara Robinson. Harper, 1972.

What if several children who have never heard the Christmas story decide to put on a Christmas pageant? The Herdman kids not only produce a hilarious unique version of the play (their interpretation of the roles is based on *Amazing Comics*) but also learn the real meaning of Christmas. The dress rehearsal is a disaster; but on opening night the Herdman touches are interesting, even provocative.

Bunnicula: A Rabbit-Tale of Mystery, by Deborah and James Howe. Atheneum, 1979.

The dog Harold and Chester the cat investigate the mystery of the cute little bunny Bunnicula. Could he be a vampire? White vegetables are suspicious—even the Monroe family thinks so. Will a pendant of garlic save Harold and Chester? They do try a more daring tactic to ward off vampires—a "sharp steak" to the heart— and Mrs. Monroe decides that all the pets need to go to the veterinarian.

Hank the Cowdog, by John R. Erickson. Maverick, 1983.

Hank the Cowdog, head of ranch security (or so he thinks), investigates all kinds of trouble on the ranch with the help of Drover, a little dog who's smarter than he looks. Hank turns a run-in with the coyotes to his advantage, using it as a way to escape (or so he hopes); but the coyotes decide he should join them! That puts Drover in charge at the ranch. When the coyotes decide to raid the ranch, Hank has to decide where and with whom he belongs.

How to Eat Fried Worms, by Thomas Rockwell. Watts, 1973.

What if you made a bet to eat one worm a day for several days? Would you do it if it would pay for a minibike? You can eat worms fried, with catsup, on a sandwich, or raw, for example. If you think you can stomach this book, read on.

Soup, by Robert Newton Peck. Knopf, 1974.

Did you ever have a friend who dared you to do something, then was never around when you got into trouble for it? Then meet Soup. Take the matter of his instruction on how to roll downhill in a barrel: balance your weight. It was impossible, and *I* landed in the hencoop. So why am I happy? He is my friend.

Where the Sidewalk Ends, by Shel Silverstein. Harper, 1974.

These not-so-traditional poems express the feelings and thoughts you really have, not those you're supposed to have. No mush here! They will make you laugh—sometimes even at yourself.

I Want a Book about Little People

Among the Dolls, by William Sleator. Dutton, 1975.

Vicki becomes part of the eerie world of the dolls in her antique dollhouse and must deal with their meanness and revenge. Dandaroo, the youngest doll, agrees to help her find the lost doll so that Vicki can escape to her own home and return to her original size. She is delighted when her parents sell the dollhouse!

Awfully Short for the Fourth Grade, by Elvira Woodruff. Holiday, 1989.

Noah loves to play with his plastic miniature action figures. Then he discovers a magic powder that makes the toys come alive and reduces him to their size. Now he can share in their adventures, which involve avoiding grown-ups stomping about, a hamster, chewing gum, and the hazards of the larger world, in places such as Noah's school.

The Borrowers, by Mary Norton. Harcourt, 1952.

When things disappear or are misplaced, you can be sure the Borrowers have them. No bigger than pencils, these tiny people who live under the floor find new uses for the objects that once belonged to human beings. However, they must always be careful not to be seen by the humans who share their world.

The Dollhouse Caper, by Jean S. O'Connell. Crowell, 1975.

When the Dollhouse family overhears a conversation between two burglars who are planning to rob the Human family's house, they try to think of a way to help the family. How can they get the message across to the boys in the family, especially when they, the

Dollhouse family, can only come to life in the absence of humans—be they family or burglars! Mr. Dollhouse times their plan just right.

Good-bye Pink Pig, by C. S. Adler. Putnam, 1985.

Pink Pig, made of quartz and as small as a lima bean, is Amanda's favorite miniature. While holding the pig, she is able to go to the little world, where she can escape her unhappy life. When Wizard brings desolation to the little world, Amanda confronts and destroys him to save Pink Pig and the others. Her brother Dale helps her deal realistically with her problems, and she puts Pink Pig back on the shelf.

The Indian in the Cupboard, by Lynne Reid Banks. Doubleday, 1980.

Patrick gives Omri a small second-hand plastic Indian on his ninth birthday. Omri also receives a metal cupboard, and he locates a tiny key, of similar vintage, which will unlock it. Imagine his surprise when, after locking the Indian inside the cupboard, he hears a tiny voice and tapping sounds coming from within. The miniature toy, Little Bear, has come alive! Other figures also become real. Patrick and Omri enjoy them and are sad when the figures change back into their old plastic forms.

King of the Dollhouse, by Patricia Clapp. Lothrop, 1974.

Ellie, somewhat lonesome during her summer vacation, is delighted to have King Borra Borra and his children come to occupy her dollhouse. She immediately becomes busy fulfilling the king's requests, satisfying the children's appetites for peanut butter, and keeping her guests hidden from her mother. When Ellie goes back to school, they cannot exist without her and must leave. The king very properly sends a thank-you note and a gift to her.

Mindy's Mysterious Miniature, by Jane Louise Curry. Harcourt, 1970.

Mindy is enchanted by the well-furnished dollhouse she buys at an auction. There is something unusual about it, especially when a strange man comes snooping around her mother's antique shop asking about doll furniture. Then Mrs. Bright, her neighbor, discovers that the dollhouse looks exactly like her own childhood home. Suddenly, Mindy and Mrs. Bright find themselves inside the dollhouse! Is this a simple shrink-and-unshrink story? Hardly.

I Don't Like to Read, But I Have to Do a Book Report . . .

Babe, the Gallant Pig, by Dick King-Smith. Crown, 1983.

Farmer Hogget correctly guesses the weight of a pig and wins it. He decides to keep it with Fly and her puppies, and the pig seems happy. That is how a wise old sheep dog comes to teach her adopted piglet new tricks, and Babe becomes a champion sheep pig!

The Castle in the Attic, by Elizabeth Winthrop. Holiday, 1985.

Mrs. Phillips gives William a miniature castle because she is leaving the family, having been with them since William was born. To William's amazement, the Silver Knight, a small figure inside the castle, comes to life. When they discover how that happened, William and Mrs. Phillips shrink to the knight's size to help him. Their adventure is meant to delay Mrs. Phillips's departure, which William dreads, but the real world comes back to be dealt with somewhat more easily after their success in the fantasy world.

Hatchet, by Gary Paulsen. Bradbury, 1987.

Surviving in the Canadian wilderness with no other tool but a hatchet is Brian's foremost concern after the plane crash. Only thirteen, he makes mistakes, one of which is to drop the hatchet in the lake! He learns a lot, too; and one thing he learns is patience.

The Indian in the Cupboard, by Lynne Reid Banks. Doubleday, 1980.

With the turn of a key, Omri can magically bring to life the three-inch Indian figure he placed inside his cupboard on the evening of his birthday, but anyone so small needs protection. He and his friend Patrick find companions for Little Bear and try to take care of all of the miniatures without attracting attention—not an easy feat when the Indian shoots the cowboy and wants to marry the girl!

Stinker from Space, by Pamela F. Service. Scribner, 1988.

When his spaceship crashes in America, an injured alien is forced to switch to the only available host body—that of a skunk! His mind is far superior to that of a skunk, however; and he is soon making plans to return to his own planet!

Trapped in Death Cave, by Bill Wallace. Holiday, 1984.

When Gary and Brian try to find Grandpa's killer, the lost treasure, and the Snake Dancer's Gold, Gary is kidnapped, and Brian asks Mrs. Becker to help him. She knows the location of Snake Dancer's Cave, which the Indians call Death Cave. In the cave Brian hears Gary's voice but not soon enough to save himself from falling into the pit with him. This is just the beginning of a series of dangers, and eventually the boys learn why the cave has two names.

I Want That Story about How, in the End, They All Become Real

Alexander and the Wind-Up Mouse, by Leo Lionni. Pantheon, 1969.

Alexander is a real mouse, and he is tired of hearing people scream when they see him. He wishes he could become a wind-up mouse like his friend Willy and be cuddled and loved—until he finds Willy in a box of old toys to be discarded. Then Alexander knows that only the magic lizard spell can come to the rescue. However, what should Alexander wish for: to become a wind-up mouse like Willy—or for Willy to become a real mouse like Alexander?

The Mouse and His Child, by Russell Hoban. Harper, 1967.

When they were new, the wind-up mouse and his clockwork child once danced in a circle under the Christmas tree. Now their gears have jammed as the result of an accident, and they find themselves in the trash. An old tramp who is rummaging through the garbage can pulls them out and repairs their mechanism as best he can. Then he sets them on a marvelous quest: to discover the secret of becoming self-winding.

The Return of the Twelves, by Pauline Clarke. Dell, 1986.

Max knows the noises in the attic aren't coming from rats or birds. The first time he goes into the attic, he finds a group of wooden figurines. Old and battered, their paint wearing thin, the figurines were carefully hidden under the floorboards. They are soldiers from the time of Napoleon, and there are twelve of them. But the best thing about them is the secret that only Max discovers: for *him* the twelve wooden soldiers can come alive.

The Story of Pygmalion, by Pamela Espeland. Carolrhoda, 1981.

The ancient Cyprian sculptor Pygmalion vows never to lose his heart to a woman or to marry. However, when he creates a beautiful lifelike marble statue of a woman, he falls in love with it. Unfortunately, a lifeless figure of stone can never return a human being's love, so Pygmalion prays to Venus, the goddess of love, to aid him in his seemingly hopeless plight.

The Sugar Prince, by Fiona Moodie. Adama, 1987.

Spoiled princess Geraldine would rather marry one of her own dolls than a real human prince, but her father is insistent: The princess must marry. So Geraldine commands the royal cook to make a life-size doll out of sugar to be her Prince Charming. "Isn't he sweet?" she cries in delight, as she drags her doll husband around with her everywhere. How her subjects laugh at the foolish princess! But Geraldine doesn't care—she doesn't, at least, until one day her sugar prince comes to life.

The Velveteen Rabbit, by Margery Williams. Knopf, 1983.

Wise old Skin Horse says that only a child's love can make a nursery toy Real. Rabbit longs to become like the furry, brown brand-new rabbits that frolic in the bracken outside the nursery at night; but when Boy recovers from his bout with scarlet fever, Rabbit learns that, in the morning, he and all Boy's old books and toys will be burned to prevent reinfection. That night Rabbit becomes Real to everyone.

Do You Have Books on the Holocaust?

The Children We Remember, by Chana Byers Abells. Greenwillow, 1983.

A tribute to the children of the Holocaust—to both the victims and the survivors—these photographs, with very brief text, first show the children in school and at play during the years before the war and then show them under Nazi rule, living under the worst of conditions or escaping from those conditions. The survivors go on to raise children of their own to be like "the children we remember."

The Devil's Arithmetic, by Jane Yolen. Viking, 1988.

Hannah Stern is tired of being reminded about events in Jewish history and especially about her grandfather's loss of his family in the Holocaust. However, a strange thing happens during the Passover seder at his home: Twelve-year-old Hannah finds herself in Poland in 1940 as one of millions of prisoners being sent to a concentration camp. Remembering *is* important, she learns, when she returns to the present and shares memories with her Aunt Eva, who was in the same camp.

Number the Stars, by Lois Lowry. Houghton, 1989.

In a test of friendship and courage, Annemarie's family assists in hiding Ellen Rosen and her family when the Nazis begin deportation of all the Jews from Denmark. The entire country, from the king on down, helps the Jews hide and then escape to safety in Sweden.

Rose Blanche, by Roberto Innocenti. Creative Education, 1985.

The arrival of Nazi soldiers in her small German town changes Rose Blanche's life forever. Secretly following the route taken by an army truck, she discovers a concentration camp where there are starving children. She sneaks back to the camp with food for the prisoners as often as she can. As she stands at the fence, surprised that all the prisoners are gone, there is a shot; and she does not survive to see the other soldiers come or the end of the war.

The Upstairs Room, by Johanna Reiss. Crowell, 1972.

Like Anne Frank, Annie is a Jewish girl living in Holland during World War II. She and her sister Sini go into hiding on a farm, and for more than two years they stay in an upstairs room, waiting for the time when they will again be safe and free. During this period they celebrate birthdays and do exercises, talking about whether the war will end in time for them to enjoy their youth under normal circumstances.

We Remember the Holocaust, by David A. Adler. Holt, 1989.

The people interviewed tell about pre-Nazi Germany and about the concentration camps, where during the years between 1933 and 1945 an estimated six million Jews were slaughtered. Their stories are backed up by graphic photographs.

I Want a Book about Kids

AT HOME

Angel's Mother's Wedding, by Judy Delton. Houghton, 1987.

With all she has learned about weddings from her best friend Edna, Angel is sure her mother and future stepfather, a television clown, are not doing enough planning for the event. Her worrying is not of any help in solving the real problems that happen at the last minute. The suit for the groom doesn't arrive from the cleaners, while the suit that does arrive by express mail for Rags, her brother, leaves him terribly disappointed; it doesn't match his idea of what a "ring bear" should wear.

Between Friends, by Sheila Garrigue. Bradbury, 1978.

When she and her family move to New England from California, Jill learns that one of their neighbors is mentally retarded. Both Jill and her mother are afraid the baby her mother is expecting will be retarded like Dede. In spite of her mother's and friends' disapproval, Jill gradually becomes friendly with Dede, who unexpectedly helps Jill through a difficult situation.

Circle of Gold, by Candy Dawson Boyd. Scholastic, 1984.

Mattie and Matt are twins. Their life seems to be going downhill since their father's death, although their mother is working at two jobs to keep them financially afloat. Mattie thinks that a pin of gold with a pearl will focus attention on—and in some way help them all to get out of—the unhappiness now apparent in their household. It does since Mattie attempts to write an essay to win the prize money to pay for it. Each family member achieves an important victory that increases their security: Mattie is victorious over Angel,

who accuses Mattie of stealing her bracelet; Matt succeeds at basketball tryouts; and Mama lands a two-year contract to manage the
apartment house.

A Family Apart, by Joan Lowery Nixon. Bantam, 1987.

When their father dies, the six Kelly children, aged six to thirteen, three boys and three girls, are sent in 1860 by their mother on
one of the orphan trains from New York City to Missouri farms,
where they will be put to work. They are not orphans, and they
cannot understand their mother's decision, which will also separate
the children from one another. Frances, the oldest, promises her
mother she will try to keep Petey, the youngest, by her side, but she
has to pretend to be a boy to do so.

Henry, by Nina Bawden. Lothrop, 1988.

It is probably a lucky thing when Charlie knocks a baby red
squirrel out of his nest with a slingshot. The family, evacuated from
London to Wales during World War II, focuses on raising Henry
(the squirrel) and providing him with food, shelter, and love while
their father is in the navy. Henry and the three children adjust to
their new surroundings despite the war.

Like Jake and Me, by Mavis Jukes. Knopf, 1984.

Alex and his stepfather, Jake, seem very different. Jake is a
strong cowboy while Alex likes ballet and is too chicken to pull out
his loose tooth. However, it's Alex to the rescue when a terrified
Jake thinks a wolf spider is in his clothes. Because she is pregnant,
Alex's mother is pleased to see that the tooth has come out and that
the two are acting so friendly.

Mariah Keeps Cool, by Mildred Pitts Walter. Bradbury, 1990.

Denise is sixteen, closer in age to her new stepsister Lynn than
to Mariah, who is eleven. Denise is *his* daughter, but their daddy does
not back down on the rules a family must observe if it wants to exist as
a unit. Neither parent is unfair or unsupportive; it just takes Mariah
longer than Lynn to become accustomed to Denise; and Denise, left
without many alternatives, is really reluctant to fit in smoothly.

Oh, Brother, by Johnniece Marshall Wilson. Scholastic, 1988.

As they grow up, Alex and Andrew seem to grow apart.
Andrew uses Alex's bike without telling him and with seemingly
no thought of the hardship it places on Alex, who delivers papers.
Their parents scold, but it gets worse, as the bike is stolen from

Andrew, and Alex suspects that Andrew has stolen money from him. Alex finally hears Andrew's side of the story, and Andrew confesses to him that he was probably jealous of his younger brother, who has a steadier nature and finishes whatever he sets out to do. Alex realizes that his older brother is not mean, only trying to be independent; and a sort of truce follows.

Piggybook, by Anthony Browne. Knopf, 1986.

Mr. Piggott and his sons are decidedly chauvinistic. Leaving a cryptic note, "You are pigs," Mrs. Piggott disappears, leaving them to fend for themselves. Their slovenly behavior literally takes over, and pigs they do become. When Mom returns, she is happy; and you may already guess why.

A Secret Friend, by Marilyn Sachs. Doubleday, 1978.

When her best friend Wendy turns against her, Jessica can hardly bear it. Her efforts to make Wendy be friends with her again only seem to make things worse. Furthermore, her usually happy relationship with her mother is becoming more and more complicated, and daily notes from a secret friend confuse things all the more.

Split Sisters, by C. S. Adler. Macmillan, 1986.

Case thinks her older sister Jen is just about perfect and never wants to be away from her. She also loves the house in Stamford and her stepfather, Gerry. So when her mother decides she and Gerry should separate, Case is faced with the prospect of living on a boat with Gerry and of being separated from both Jen and their house. Case is still hoping the family will stay together when Jen leaves for computer camp and she and her grandmother go to New York for a week, leaving their parents—alone.

Superfudge, by Judy Blume. Dutton, 1980.

Peter's four-year-old brother, known as Fudge, uses lots of big words (like *catastrophe*), and he even knows where babies come from; but he still causes Peter lots of trouble. The mere thought of another baby in the family is enough to make Peter want to leave home. Things get worse when Dad announces the family is moving. Much to Peter's surprise, Princeton, New Jersey, has its good points, and even his baby sister Tootsie can be fun sometimes.

Switcharound, by Lois Lowry. Houghton, 1985.

If their mother and the law say they have to go, J. P. and

Caroline will spend the summer with Dad and his new wife, Lillian, and their family in Des Moines. The switcharounds are numerous: Caroline is better suited to coaching baseball than to taking care of the twin babies; and J. P., who doesn't like baseball and is a computer nut, helps his father, who is a baseball fan but doesn't understand the computer in his store. Caroline switches the twins and then finds one is allergic to the other's medicine, but she cannot bring herself to tell Lillian what she has done. The summer they thought they would hate gets all switched around, too; at the end of it, they actually like Des Moines.

Thatcher Payne-in-the-Neck, by Betty Bates. Holiday, 1985.

Kimberly Slocum and Thatcher Payne are good friends, and they more or less arrange the marriage of her dad and his mother during summer vacation. Perhaps they should have realized that Hugo, Thatcher's dog, will play a large role. When the dog destroys her leaf album, Kim runs away because she feels left out in her new family and at the new school. Thatcher is the one who knows where to find her, and he spots a leaf on the way back that they agree will be a good one for a new leaf book. They are not only brother and sister now but they are also best friends again.

When the Boys Ran the House, by Joan Carris. Lippincott, 1982.

Jut is the oldest and only thirteen, but he is in charge while his father is in Europe on a business trip and their mother is convalescing at home. Nick, seven years old, and Marty, ten, quarrel a lot; Gus is two! The family holds together primarily because Nurse "Amazon" Brown, who comes part time, can also coach Jut in basketball before tryouts and usually takes them all someplace special on Saturday afternoons. Marty develops a knack for cooking, and Jut never gives up—not, at least, until his father is home.

IN SCHOOL

Anastasia Krupnik, by Lois Lowry. Houghton, 1979.

Anastasia is definitely different from everyone in her class, because she loves cold spinach sandwiches and hates green ice cream. To keep track of all the things she loves and hates, she carries a green notebook, carefully marking out and adding things to her two lists. When her parents announce that a new baby is on the way, Anastasia definitely knows that this is on her hate list, or is it?

Breadsticks and Blessing Places, by Candy Dawson Boyd. Macmillan, 1985.

Toni, Mattie, Raymond, and Susan are friends who are expected to go on to the best college preparatory school in Chicago after middle school; and with the exception of Susan, who doesn't really care about school, they study for the admission tests. Susan is hit by a car, and Toni's difficulty in coming to terms with Susan's death alarms Toni's friends and parents. However, Mattie, who faced her own father's death the year before, helps Toni; and by the time she receives the results of the tests, Toni is feeling more equal to the situations in her life.

Charlotte Cheetham: Master of Disaster, by Barbara Ware Holmes. Harper, 1985.

Being popular in school is the one thing Charlotte Cheetham, a fifth-grader, wants most and the one thing that constantly eludes her. In order to win the favor of the most popular girl in the class, Charlotte blurts out an incredible lie that she knows she can't get away with. In order to cover up the first lie, she has to keep inventing new ones. The lie about the sticker factory is the one she feels she can never undo, and it does have quite an effect on her personality, attitude, and new activity.

Class Clown, by Johanna Hurwitz. Morrow, 1987.

Unhappy with his image as an unruly and obnoxious third-grader, Lucas Scott decides to change his ways; but this isn't as easy as he first thought. His enthusiasm and energy often get him into trouble, especially when he has the best intentions. An exasperated teacher and a harried mother still have faith in him after his performance in the cultural arts program and in the mini-circus.

Fourth Grade Celebrity, by Patricia Reilly Giff. Delacorte, 1979.

Casey Valentine wants desperately to be a celebrity and to outshine her older sister Van. Being class president isn't enough; she decides to start a class newspaper. Nothing works, until one of her plans backfires. Casey's formula for success surprises everyone, but no one is more surprised than Casey herself.

Herbie Jones and the Class Gift, by Suzy Kline. Putnam, 1987.

Each person in the class is asked to contribute one dollar to the teacher's gift, but Herbie and his best friend, Ray, are broke! When they are given the job of picking up the package and accidentally break the gift, they have spent all but twenty-five cents of the class money. Only a miracle can save them now. Avoid smiling—if you can.

How to Survive Third Grade, by Laurie Lawlor. Whitman, 1988.
   Everything seems hopeless until Ernest tries to be friends with Jomo, a new African boy in his class. This new friendship is really secure after Jomo stands up for Ernest and Ernest invites Jomo to share the pizza he won in the All-School Balloon Send-Off.

Invisible Lissa, by Natalia Honeycutt. Bradbury, 1985.
   Lissa's little brother, Jason, disrupts the cheerleading practice that Debra organizes; and the result is hard feelings. Debra has lots of energy, with ego and money to match; she makes new friends, while Lissa loses them. Katie, Lissa's best friend, joins the lunch club Debra has started. Fairly certain that Debra destroyed her class project out of jealousy, Lissa still hopes for an invitation to FUNCHY; she no longer wants to be an outcast, and she hopes to be friends with Katie again. Will she join FUNCHY when she finds out more about it?

Nothing's Fair in Fifth Grade, by Barthe DeClements. Viking, 1981.
   Nothing is fair in the fifth grade, especially if you are the new girl in class—and overweight. Elsie, the new girl, has the dubious honor of being the class reject *and* the class thief. Nobody will have anything to do with her until her classmate Jennifer begins to feel sorry for her and brings her into her group of friends. They soon discover why Elsie needs so much attention and why appearances are deceiving.

Teacher's Pet, by Johanna Hurwitz. Morrow, 1988.
   Cricket loves being the teacher's pet, but her enthusiasm fades when she finds out the fourth-grade teacher does not play favorites. To make matters worse, Zoe, a new girl in the class, is competing with Cricket to be the best student. It never occurs to Cricket that she and her rival will have the same idea—to hunt for the teacher's lost cat. When they decide to hunt together, they find the wrong cat, of course; but that's okay with them. How does their teacher react?

Thirteen Ways to Sink a Sub, by Jamie Gilson. Lothrop, 1982.
   It's the boys against the girls to see who can shake up the substitute teacher (make her cry). The only problem is that this "sub" is not sinking! The lost-contact-lens routine and the snow-

balls don't phase her at all. It's going to be tough for the losers in Room 4B.

IN TROUBLE

Among the Dolls, by William Sleator. Dutton, 1975.

Mysteriously reduced to doll-size, Vicki tries desperately to escape the vindictive dolls in her antique dollhouse. The attic holds the secret to her escape, if only she can outwit her menacing captors and reach the stairs. She wants to save Dandaroo, the youngest doll, who has helped her understand how the attic fits into her real-life problems.

Blood in the Snow, by Marlene Fanta Shyer. Houghton, 1975.

When Max finds a young silver fox terrified and slowly dying in a steel-jaw trap, he faces a hard decision, because he doesn't have the strength to pry open the trap, even when the fox lets him near enough to try.

Charlie Pippin, by Candy Dawson Boyd. Macmillan, 1987.

Charlie, who is eleven years old, becomes very interested in a school project on the Vietnam War and works with her friends to complete it. Although her father served in the war, he never talks about it; and the situation seems to lead to a general antagonism between them. She is angry because he turns up by surprise at a contest, unnerving her as she makes a speech on peace, in which she uses material on Vietnam. Her father is angry because she lies to everyone in order to go with her Uncle Ben to Washington, D.C. Both of these matters pave the way for the moment when Charlie and her father are able to communicate without anger and when she can ask questions she had never before dared to.

I Want to Go Home! by Gordon Korman. Scholastic, 1981.

His parents have been advised by the school guidance department that Rudy needs to go to camp but that he may have a negative attitude when he gets there. Indeed he does. He is determined to escape this month of fun (punishment). He finds a cohort, Mike Webster; and soon the counselors run out of real ways to punish them! What next? Yes, Rudy takes a turn as camp director.

Last Look, by Clyde Robert Bulla. Crowell, 1979.

Rhoda, the new girl at Madame Vere's summer school, is jealous of Monica and tricks her into coming to a haunted house. She pushes Monica, and they both fall into an empty well. No one is hurt. School goes on, with a new girl taking Rhoda's place when Rhoda is sent back to her mother, and Monica sees life differently now.

The Mariah Delany Lending Library Disaster, by Sheila Greenwald. Houghton, 1977.

Mariah decides to start her own library in the neighborhood. The problem is that she is lending out her family's books without their knowing. Mariah likes her newest enterprise very much until she realizes that the books are not being returned; and she is forced to become a collection agent, especially so that she can retrieve her mother's cookbooks and her father's leather-bound set of Dickens.

Steady, Freddie! by Scott Corbett. Dutton, 1970.

Donna finds a frog, which she instantly names Freddie, in her shoulder bag after a trip to the zoo. She quickly packs him into a box of Girl Scout cookies to hide him until she can take him to a swamp! In the general mix-up Freddie may die of suffocation and must be retrieved for a number of other reasons.

Storm Boy, by Colin Thiele. Harper, 1963.

His father is a beachcomber, and Fingerbone, an Australian aborigine, is a friend who lives nearby. Mr. Percival is a pelican that will not return to the sanctuary, preferring to live with Storm Boy, who is eleven. Storm Boy's grief over the vicious death of his pet pelican will be better eased if he chooses to leave his home for boarding school; and his expenses are to be covered by the sailors, whom he and Mr. Percival had saved from drowning.

They Called Me Leni, by Zdenka Bezdekova. Bobbs-Merrill, 1973.

Abducted and raised in Germany by the Nazis, Leni hears whispers about her true family and is determined to find her real parents. She locates her old suitcase in the attic and takes it with her for any clues to her identity when she goes to the Child Welfare Department of the United Nations Relief and Rehabilitation Administration. There, American soldiers check the files but cannot find her listed as missing under the name Leni. However, there is an Alena; and there is sufficient proof to convince Leni that she and Alena are the same person. Her mother is alive and living in Czechoslovakia, and Leni will have to learn to say "Mummy" in Czech.

What Happened in Hamelin, by Gloria Skurzynski. Four Winds, 1979.

The rats have just come to Hamelin, and the crops have been spoiled by rain for two years. The people are starved for music, and everyone enjoys the flute music of the piper, a stranger, on his second day in the town on June 6, 1284. Throughout the month, Albert, the baker's helper, sees the strategy evolve. He helps the sinister Pied Piper of Hamelin to lure 130 children to their mysterious end on June 26. At the last minute he must decide whether to go with the stranger as his assistant.

IN WORSE TROUBLE

The Goats, by Brock Cole. Farrar, 1987.

Laura and Howie are strangers and outcasts at summer camp. A cruel prank by the other campers strands them on a deserted island one night without their clothes. After they manage to leave the island, taking or finding food and clothes, they stick together, determined to maintain a way to accommodate their friendship.

Hatchet, by Gary Paulsen. Bradbury, 1987.

During a trip to visit his father, the pilot of Brian's plane dies, and the plane crashes. His parents' divorce recedes in his mind as he faces a more immediate reality: He must learn to survive alone in the wilderness.

Mystery of Hurricane Castle, by Joan Lowery Nixon. Criterion, 1964.

As a hurricane approaches, Kathy and Maureen are forced to take shelter in a haunted old castle. Danny, their brother, brings his teddy bear Todey. Kathy wants to explore the castle to see if anyone lives there; Maureen thinks they shouldn't, because it might be haunted. When Danny disappears, however, they have to go upstairs.

Nightmare Island, by Ron Roy. Dutton, 1981.

An overnight camping trip turns into a nightmare for two brothers when the island where they are camping becomes a raging inferno. Although warned against making fires on the island, Harley fails to consider an oil spill on the surface of the water around the island, and an enormous fire starts. Scoop, his younger brother, struggles to see through the billowing smoke to find the rocks they had climbed in the afternoon. They make their way there, but do not find the expected cave, and now they are exhausted.

Nightmare Mountain, by Peg Kehret. Dutton, 1989.

Molly anticipates an enjoyable month on a llama farm in the mountains of Washington with her Aunt Karen, although this is the first time she will be meeting her aunt's husband, Phil, and his son Glendon. Her mother is in Japan on a business trip, and Molly soon wishes she would come home—and that she would make it fast. The circumstances are iffy—a possible poisoning, a stolen llama, and a bale of hay that falls from the loft. Is she in danger from her own step-cousin? An avalanche puts them on the same side but is an ordeal they barely survive.

On My Honor, by Marion Dane Bauer. Clarion, 1986.

Disobeying their parents, Joel and Tony go swimming in the river—with tragic results. When Joel discovers that Tony is not behind him as they race for the sandbar, he goes back, where he dives four times for Tony; the driver of a passing car also tries to find Tony but fails. Joel must now return home; but why doesn't he tell them that Tony is dead and give an account of how it happened?

The Terrible Wave, by Marden Dahlstedt. Coward, 1972.

In the flash flood of 1889 in Johnstown, Pennsylvania, Megan Maxwell is pushed out into the water when the wave hits their house. After being rescued, she sets out to find her family. She locates first their cook and then her father, who can account for the others. Then she feels she must return to find those with whom she was rescued—especially a child who cannot speak—and then give assistance through the newly formed Red Cross.

LIKE ME

The Cat Ate My Gymsuit, by Paula Danziger. Delacorte, 1974.

Marcy Lewis hates everything—her father, her school, her appearance—until a new English teacher with different teaching methods takes an interest in her and other students and encourages her to develop her talents and to become independent. You'll see Marcy change from a "blimp" to a witty and secure adolescent, willing to fight for her teacher's reinstatement.

The Flunking of Joshua T. Bates, by Susan Shreve. Knopf, 1984.

At first Joshua is horrified at having to repeat third grade. However, his best friend, Arthur, helps on the playground, and his new teacher, Mrs. Goodwin, treats him like he is the best student in third grade and zeros in on his reading problem, tutoring him after school. Things turn out better after all—and sooner than he thought.

The Great Ideas of Lila Fenwick, by Kate McMullan. Dial, 1986.

Fifth-grader Lila Fenwick has great ideas—sometimes. If nothing else, her ideas are entertaining. When the class pet, Chocolate, a Brazilian guinea pig, disappears, Lila appoints herself to find him. In order to find a guinea pig, Lila decides, you have to think like one, but crawling around on hands and knees with a wrinkled-up nose produces only laughs for poor Lila. Chocolate is found alive and well—and has become a mother. The guinea-pig incident is only one of her escapades; others are a Halloween party, a museum trip for the entire class, and the Fifth Grade Girls' Spring Weekend at the end of the school year.

Herbie Jones and Hamburger Head, by Suzy Kline. Putnam, 1989.

Herbie Jones is a third-grader who wants a dog more than anything else in the world. Even Herbie's best friend Ray has a dog; but Herbie's dad refuses to give in. One hot day, when Herbie sees a dog in a car with the windows rolled up and Herbie, Ray, and the dog accidentally prevent a bank robbery, Mr. Jones relents a bit on the idea of having a dog around. Poor Hamburger Head (an apt but hastily chosen name) isn't the prettiest dog in the world; but he does like the right baseball team (the Yankees) and spaghetti.

Hobie Hanson, Greatest Hero of the Mall, by Jamie Gilson. Lothrop, 1989.

Hobie Hanson is baby-sitting with Toby, his neighbor, when a sudden storm floods the town. He sees an opportunity to become a hero by rescuing Toby and his own cat Fido; but he drops his plan to sail away on a picnic table when Molly Bosco arrives in her inflatable giraffe—which doesn't do much to boost Hobie's self-esteem. To make matters worse, he has neglected to rescue a pair of diamond earrings! When his class moves to a temporary location in the local mall, Hobie gets one more chance to become a hero.

Muggie Maggie, by Beverly Cleary. Morrow, 1990.

Maggie becomes Muggie when she defies, on the basis of her ability already to print and to use her father's computer, the teacher's instruction on how to do cursive writing in third grade. (With cursive writing you have to pay attention to which loops to close or leave open.) Her resistance finally breaks down when she realizes she cannot read cursive writing. She is forced to do a fast catch-up to reach the level of her classmates.

Nutty for President, by Dean Hughes. Atheneum, 1981.

William Bilks, child prodigy and new student, wants Nutty (Frederick Nutsell) to run for student-body president so he can be his campaign manager. He realizes he must change Nutty's image from practical joker to student representative; Nutty is sometimes cooperative but does not want to be a puppet. Angela, a sixth-grader and the first girl to be nominated, is a real contender; but Nutty considers dropping out of the race, mainly so that he can revert to his old spontaneous self.

Sixth Grade Can Really Kill You, by Barthe DeClements. Viking, 1985.

Helen recognizes some of the pupils in Mrs. Lobb's sixth-grade class from spending previous years in school with them; and they know her, too, as she often gets discipline slips, sets off firecrackers, plays softball well, does math easily, but reads at a second-grade level. Her mother refuses to sign the papers that would permit the school to give her special reading instruction. Then comes the ultimatum—she must improve her reading or she will not be promoted to junior high school. An understanding uncle, a new classroom teacher, and her father's intervention all help her adjust to the remedial reading class, and soon she is making real progress.

There's a Boy in the Girls' Bathroom, by Louis Sachar. Knopf, 1987.

As a new kid in school, Jeff Fishkin has no choice in where he sits in Mrs. Ebbel's class; the only vacant place is last seat, last row, next to Bradley Chalkers, the class bad boy who never does his homework and does his best to make the rest of the class miserable. Carla, the kind and sensitive new counselor, is helping Jeff and Bradley to form a special off-again on-again friendship. It helps that both of them have received black eyes in situations they are not pleased about. Then Carla is transferred.

Where Does the Teacher Live? by Paula Kurzband Feder. Dutton, 1979.

No one has really ever stopped to consider where Mrs. Greengrass, their teacher, lives. Nancy thinks all teachers live at school; but Willie, the smartest boy in class, knows that isn't right. Nancy, Willie, and Alba watch for four days and can't figure why she goes home in different vehicles, so they ask her. She asks them to wait for her after school, and still another type of vehicle appears to pick her up—an ice-cream truck driven by her uncle. They all get treated to ice cream, but he takes *them* home first. Where *does* she live?

ON THEIR OWN

Fair's Fair, by Leon Garfield. Doubleday, 1981.

One snowy day, Jackson, an orphan, shares his hot meat pie with a stray dog. He is surprised to find a house key under the dog's collar. What door will the key fit? The *right* door is a mansion's. Should he venture inside? Why not; he's brought their dog home, and he's cold. The dog's owner is not home; but he and a little girl, Lillipolly, who has arrived under similar circumstances, do only house chores, because food arrives at the door every morning. They decide to wait until Christmas when surely the family will come home, but instead a man who wants a family comes by himself. Fortunately, they measure up to his expectations.

A Girl Called Boy, by Belinda Hurmence. Houghton, 1982.

She is eleven years old, her nickname is Boy, and she's a spit-fire. Her real name is Blanche Overtha Yancey, after her two grand-mothers. Her ancestors may have been slaves, but she contends nobody could have made her a slave! One day in the wilderness of North Carolina, she flounces away from a picnic and gets lost. And lost in time, too; it's 1853, and slave catchers are after her! She returns with a deep cut on her face and a lot of respect for the Yancey family heritage.

Guys from Space, by Daniel Pinkwater. Macmillan, 1989.

A boy is standing in his backyard when something big lands beside him. Guys step out of the spaceship and ask the boy if he wants to take a ride. He explains that he will have to ask his mother; they tell him he needs a space helmet. He is back in time for supper— having had a good time!

The Half-A-Moon Inn, by Paul Fleischman. Harper, 1980.

Lost in the forest, searching for his mother who has not re-turned from her monthly trek to the market, Aaron rides with a ragman, who never admits he cannot read and never understands that Aaron cannot speak. He reaches Half-A-Moon Inn and stum-bles right into Miss Grackle's evil system of thieving! When his mother passes by, Aaron is unable to tell her he is there, although he tries by relettering the sign over the inn door. It takes a blizzard, a curse on a dishonest person (for whom a fire won't light), and a handkerchief to set in motion his return home.

Help! Let Me Out! by David Lord Porter. Houghton, 1982.

Hugo sends in for the special offer *How to Become a Ventriloquist!* The book arrives, and the first day he learns how to throw his voice. The problem is that Hugo's voice will not come back! It wanders the world having a good time while Hugo wanders the world in silent misery, trying to be cured by a trip to Paris with his parents. His voice eventually does return. How? By telegram!

Left Behind, by Carol Carrick. Clarion, 1988.

The ride on the subway to the aquarium is exciting; but on the way home, Christopher gets separated from his partner, and the class goes on without him. He is left alone standing in the crowd on the platform. Lost and very scared, he does the right thing.

Searching for Shona, by Margaret J. Anderson. Knopf, 1978.

Wealthy, parentless, unhappy Marjorie becomes friends with Shona, a brash, raggedy girl from an orphanage. World War II has just started, and the children of Great Britain are being sent away for safety. Slated to go to unknown relatives in Canada, Marjorie impulsively switches places with Shona and goes instead to live with two middle-aged sisters in the village of Canobie. Six years later, the girls meet again in Edinburgh; Shona is just back from Canada, and Marjorie is starting her training as a doctor. Having identified Shona's parents, Marjorie wants to tell her about them, but Shona doesn't want to see Marjorie or hear anything about her parents.

The Talking Eggs, retold by Robert D. San Souci. Dial, 1989.

Poor hungry Blanche meets a magical old woman in the woods and gives her a drink of water. The woman offers her a choice between two gifts: plain eggs or golden eggs encrusted with jewels. Which should Blanche take? She wants the jeweled eggs, but she follows the old woman's directions and takes only those that say "take me," the plain eggs; and she is glad she did!

Tom Thumb, retold by Richard Jesse Watson. Harcourt, 1989.

A wee boy created magically for a childless couple, Tom Thumb grows older but no larger. Tom has narrow escapes from large things, makes friends with animals, and turns up at King Arthur's court, where he is an entertainer who becomes a knight because he knows how to calm the giant Grumbong, who threatens the kingdom.

Travelers by Night, by Vivien Alcock. Delacorte, 1983.

Charlie and Belle, cousins and best friends, have *problems*. The circus where they perform is broke and about to fold. Tessie, the old elephant, whom the children love, will soon be sent to the slaughterhouse. They can't allow this to happen, so they kidnap Tessie and run away. As you might imagine, this feat is hard to accomplish quietly, even though they have a plan and the instincts and experience of good circus performers.

Do You Have Any Sports Books?

Boys in the Gym, by Elizabeth Levy. Scholastic, 1990.

Cindi is planning a surprise birthday party for her older brother Jared and is having trouble keeping it a secret from him. Then, to her dismay, Jared and some of his friends join the new boys' gymnastics class that is being formed at the previously all-girls' gym where Cindi has taken lessons for many years. To top it all off, the Pinecones, the gymnastics group that Cindi and her friends have always been in together, must learn two new compulsory exercises; if they don't all pass the routines, they won't be able to move up together to the next class, and the Pinecones group will be broken up.

Mariah Keeps Cool, by Mildred Pitts Walter. Bradbury, 1990.

As summer begins, Mariah makes no effort to hide her dislike of Denise, their daddy's daughter by another marriage. The Friendly Five, she and her four best friends, decide to train and compete in swimming and diving, the first time their part of town will be represented in the city meet. When she learns that her sister Lynn is working at a shelter for the homeless, she starts plans for a surprise birthday party for her which will benefit the shelter. Denise agrees to help with the planning but does not attend the swimming finals. It is a summer that provides Mariah opportunities to keep her cool, and she spends a long time concentrating on her last dive, because she now feels it means a lot to her and her family.

Me, Mop, and the Moondance Kid, by Walter Dean Myers. Delacorte, 1988.

Three major events involve T. J., Tommy Jackson; Mop, Miss

Olivia Parish; and Tommy's younger brother Billy, who prefers to be called Moondance: the adoption of Mop, the winning of games for the Elks team in Little League baseball, and care of the llama after the orphanage closes. They are helped in these affairs by nuns, parents, street people, and Four Times Seven, a cat with seven toes on each foot. They all match up with their talents, or faults, to succeed, as the deadlines of summer events bear down on them.

Red-Hot Hightops, by Matt Christopher. Little, 1987.

Kelly likes to play basketball, is honest in her view of herself and situations, and would like the Eagles of Eastburg Middle School to have a good season. The red hightop sneakers that appear as a gift in her locker and fit her perfectly are a mixed blessing, as she seems to play better but understand people less in the weeks before the season ends. Does she really need that kind of boost—and the worry?

Rinehart Lifts, by R. R. Knudson. Farrar, 1980.

Zan is willing to give Rinehart one last chance to find a sport in which he can excel. He makes good grades, tends his plants, and helps Zan with her homework; but she is athletic and wants a teammate or she will have to join the Mighty Four, who have dominated all the sports every year in school. Zan discovers championship weight-lifting on television. Perfect. Rinehart agrees to get into training and begins the advanced program. Zan plans to avenge herself on the Mighty Four, who vandalized their garage gym, by staging a competition which will show off Rinehart's muscles.

S.O.R. LOSERS, by Avi. Bradbury, 1984.

South Orange River Middle School (S.O.R.) has two other soccer teams, but this one is made up of boys in the seventh grade who have not yet fulfilled the school's requirement of participation in a team sport. Their coach has never coached, the tallest boy is automatically goalie, and they practice only once before playing their first game. During their six-game season, the principal, their parents, and the school counselor give them pep talks; but the scores only get a little less lopsided. The boys do not like sports; each has ability in another field. The tension builds when the last game of the year is with a team that hasn't won any games either; and S.O.R. could avoid being the losingest team in its school's history. Knowing well his team's feelings, Ed alters their T-shirts to read the truth; and they all hope they won't be lucky and win that last game.

The Ultimate Skateboard Book, by Albert Cassorla. Running Pr., 1988.

Local skateboard experts will almost certainly find new and useful information in this book. Others will want to know about skateboarding history, equipment, and performance. Instruction on maintaining various types of skateboards in safe condition is included. Your performance styles will vary after you learn the basics and try them in competition, and new tricks are being invented all the time.

I Want a Story with History in It

ABOUT COLONIAL-TYPE STUFF

Ben and Me, a New and Astonishing Life of Benjamin Franklin as Written by His Good Mouse Amos, lately discovered, edited and illustrated by Robert Lawson. Little, 1951.

Imagine what it would be like to meet Benjamin Franklin and to be a part of his daily life. Now pretend you are a mouse in search of a job. Your name is Amos, and you locate a human who has talent but who needs help. You have found a lifelong friend, a job, and an exciting adventure!

The Corduroy Road, by Patricia Edwards Clyne. Peter Smith, 1984.

Tib is an orphan, the son of Revolutionary sympathizers; and he is sent to live with his uncle, a Tory. When Tib finds a desperately ill soldier hiding in their hayloft, he helps him to reach West Point. Tib hopes to continue on to Morristown to live with his aunt. He is asked to deliver information about General Anthony Wayne and allowed to travel the Corduroy Road, which is less likely to be cut off by the British.

The Fighting Ground, by Avi. Lippincott, 1984.

Eager to learn what fighting is all about, young Jonathan rashly joins in a Revolutionary War battle against British forces—only to be captured by Hessian mercenaries. He escapes and no longer wishes to kill anyone but is forced to lead soldiers back to kill the Hessians.

Johnny Tremain, by Esther Forbes. Houghton, 1943.

Young Johnny Tremain believes his hopes of becoming a silversmith are over when his hand is burnt by molten silver. Soon, another dream involves him in events leading up to the Boston Tea Party through his acquaintance with one of colonial America's greatest patriots and silversmiths, Paul Revere.

Phoebe and the General, by Judith Berry Griffin. Coward, 1977.

When prosperous New York tavern owner Samuel Fraunces catches wind of a plot to kill General George Washington, he asks his own thirteen-year-old daughter Phoebe to act as a spy. Phoebe must discover who is behind the plot and how they plan to accomplish their goal if she is to save both the general's life and America's hope for a successful revolution.

Six Silver Spoons, by Janette Sebring Lowrey. Harper, 1971.

The famous silversmith Paul Revere makes six silver spoons for Tim and Debby to give to their mother for her birthday. However, their mother is with their grandmother in Lexington, and they are in Boston. When their father must help move guns to new hiding places, the children decide to go on. Two British soldiers stop them at the edge of town, and they almost lose their mother's gift.

HISTORY IN IT

Nettie's Trip South, by Ann Turner. Macmillan, 1987.

Before the Civil War, Nettie's brother Lockwood, a journalist, takes her and her fourteen-year-old sister Julia to Richmond, Virginia. Nettie writes to a friend about her experiences and the sights she saw on her journey, the most memorable one being a slave auction which makes her ill and strongly impresses upon her the differences in people's lives.

Not over Ten Inches High, by Harry Levy. McGraw, 1968.

Crispus Plunkett is afraid that Sheba, his new-found dog, will not meet Boston's size requirements. It is the law in 1755: A dog cannot be more than ten inches high. When a constable catches Sheba, Crispus goes to the judge, who is both kind and clever. He explains his loneliness and his reasons for wanting a pet; he does not have a brother his age, and, because he is a chimney sweep, he has no friends. The judge orders Sheba's fur to be clipped, and she is returned to Crispus in her legally correct status.

The Slave Dancer, by Paula Fox. Bradbury, 1973.
Jessie is kidnapped off the streets of New Orleans when he is thirteen to work on a slave ship. He can play a fife, and his talent is wanted—he is ordered to play music for the slaves so they will exercise and keep their physical health on the long voyage. Jessie witnesses other horrors of the slave trade on the journey, which is interrupted by a storm that leaves him and Ras, a black boy about his age, a chance to swim to land—and to make separate journeys.

Streams to the River, Rivers to the Sea, by Scott O'Dell. Houghton, 1986.
Sacajawea is a good guide and interpreter for the explorers Meriwether Lewis and William Clark as they go from the Dakotas to the Pacific Ocean. On the journey she tells us her own story as a Shoshone wife and mother. Although Clark offers to send her and her son to St. Louis for schooling, her final decision is to remain Shoshone and to teach her son the tribe's ways.

When the World's on Fire, by Sally Edwards. Coward, 1972.
Nine-year-old Annie McGuire assists the Patriots' war efforts in 1780 by courageously blowing up the British powder magazine in Charleston, South Carolina. Because she is there every day cleaning the barracks, Annie is asked to report everything to her master, and she agrees to his plan which must look like an accident since he is already suspected of treason. Her job is to light the fire. The plan fails the first time; and she is able to face the task again only because she has received definite confirmation of her brother's death at the hands of the British.

Who Is Carrie? by James Lincoln Collier and Christopher Collier. Delacorte, 1984.
Carrie ends up working for President Washington while she is trying to elude a man who is seeking to capture her and sell her into slavery in the South. Carrie, also known as Nosey, slips away from the tavern where she works as a slave to see President Washington's inaugural parade; as she hurries back, she is kidnapped but found and released to Mr. Fraunces, her master, the famous tavern keeper in New York City, who becomes the President's stew-

ard. She tries several times to find out who she is and whether she is a freed person or a slave but can never locate the proper papers.

Wilderness Journey, by William O. Steele. Harcourt, 1953.

Flan, a sickly boy, wants to join his family, but his abilities run to reading rather than hunting, so it is convenient for him to walk along the Wilderness Trail with Chapman Green, who is delivering ammunition to French Lick, where Flan's family lives. He earns the rifle he now desires in an Indian attack and continues *alone* the last day to deliver the powder and get help for Green, who is sick with a fever.

IN ANOTHER TIME

Before the Wildflowers Bloom, by Tatyana Bylinsky. Crown, 1989.

Carmela tells about the year 1916 when she is eight and about the awful waiting at home with her brothers and sisters when there is an explosion in the mine where their father works. When their mother comes home with one boot in her hand, they know the truth about their father.

Cassie's Journey: Going West in the 1860s, by Brett Harvey. Holiday, 1988.

When Cassie's family moves from Illinois to California, it takes more than six months by covered wagon. They are looking for cheap land to farm and must endure many hardships along the way: cold weather in the mountains, mosquitoes that get in the bread, white desert sand that stings their noses, and the necessity of washing clothes in the river.

The Friendship, by Mildred D. Taylor. Dial, 1987.

In 1933 in Mississippi, black children shouldn't go into a white man's store. When they go there to get medicine for Aunt Callie, they find out why Mr. Tom Bee, their friend, dares to call store owner John Wallace by his first name, and they witness the outcome of another forbidden practice.

In the Year of the Boar and Jackie Robinson, by Bette Bao Lord. Harper, 1984.

Grandfather Wong lets his sixth grandchild choose her official name before she leaves for America (she has been called Sixth

Cousin and, familiarly, Bandit). Ten thousand miles later, Shirley Temple Wong (that was her choice) is in Brooklyn, New York, in fifth grade and doing well when Mabel introduces her to baseball. The kids call her Jackie Robinson!

The Little Riders, by Margaretha Shemin. Putnam, 1988.

Johanna loves the clock tower she sees from her window as much as her grandfather does. They live next to the church, and he takes care of the mechanism that sends the twelve knights, who ride out on horseback to music, through little doors each time the clock strikes the hour. When the riders are threatened by the Germans in World War II, Johanna helps her grandparents hide them in their home. She only sees them again when the town celebrates its liberation.

Long Meg, by Rosemary Minard. Pantheon, 1982.

At fourteen Meg is tall and a skilled sword fighter. Disguised as a boy, she manages to get aboard the *Great Harry,* an English ship which is sailing to invade France. The battle is horrible, and she is wounded and left behind—and her identity discovered. When the French attack the city, she organizes the women to defend the walls. Who knows whether Long Meg is real or whether the king's plaster cured her leg?

Lost Star, the Story of Amelia Earhart, by Patricia Lauber. Scholastic, 1988.

Her life as a pilot begins right after World War I, when she receives her first flying lessons, and in 1921 she solos. Along with a few other women fliers, Amelia Earhart starts setting records and becomes the first woman to fly across the Atlantic Ocean. In 1937 when she is forty, she and her co-pilot and navigator, Fred Noonan, mysteriously disappear while attempting to fly around the world along the equator, having covered twenty-two thousand miles in less than a month.

Number the Stars, by Lois Lowry. Houghton, 1989.

During World War II Annemarie helps her Jewish friend Ellen Rosen escape from Denmark to Sweden, away from the Nazis. Annemarie knows there is no "Great-aunt Birte," whose casket rests in the living room in accordance with the old custom; but this strategy is the beginning part of a transport system. The plan also calls for great bravery, with the least amount of talk making things more secure.

Sarah, Plain and Tall, by Patricia MacLachlan. Harper, 1985.

Caleb's and Anna's father advertises for a wife and mother; and after they have the first letter from Sarah Elizabeth Wheaton, the children begin to hope she will come and decide to stay with them in their prairie home. Sarah Wheaton comes, adjusts to the differences, and wants to stay.

THAT HAPPENED A LONG TIME AGO

Chang's Paper Pony, by Eleanor Coerr. Harper, 1988.

Chang and Grandfather Li work in the kitchen of the Gold Ditch Hotel in San Francisco, where the gold miners pull Chang's pigtail and laugh at his bowing. Without any friends, Chang dreams of owning a real pony all the more. It takes hard work, a fair and kindhearted miner named Big Pete, and luck for him to realize his dream.

Daniel's Duck, by Clyde Robert Bulla. Harper, 1979.

In a time when many things were made in the home, Daniel chooses to carve, and he spends the winter making a duck. He is badly disappointed when he takes it to the craft fair and people laugh at it, but a sincere and talented wood-carver stops him before he throws it away.

Follow the Drinking Gourd, by Jeanette Winter. Knopf, 1988.

After reading a brief introduction to the history of the underground railroad, you will become involved with the story of Peg-Leg Joe and a slave family as they escape to freedom in Canada; and you will learn how the words to the song "The Drinking Gourd" guide them north. The drinking gourd is the Big Dipper, which points to the North Star.

The Josefina Story Quilt, by Eleanor Coerr. Harper, 1986.

Faith is allowed to bring her useless pet hen Josefina on the trip to California by wagon train. Josefina is a bother, but she becomes useful, laying eggs again and cackling when robbers sneak into their camp. Faith is making a quilt that tells about the journey, and she makes one patch especially in memory of Josefina.

Old Blue, by Sibyl Hancock. Putnam, 1980.

Davy's father is the trail boss, and he lets Davy ride with them to Dodge City. He rides near the head of the herd with his favorite steer, Old Blue, the longhorn that guides the others across rivers, through blizzards, and into a circle to stop a stampede. It's Davy's idea to bell the lead steer, and Old Blue seems to like it.

A Paradise Called Texas, by Janice Jordon Shefelman. Eakin, 1983.

How wonderful to travel by ship to Texas, Mina thinks. Her father will be able to own a great deal of land there—something that is not possible in Germany, where he is the youngest son. However, the trip brings unpleasant consequences: Mina's mother dies and the company that has sold the idea to the settlers fails to deliver the promised services and supplies. But there are friends, some of them Indians, and finally a home in the beautiful hill country.

The White Stallion, by Elizabeth Shub. Greenwillow, 1982.

Hot and bored with riding in the back of the family's covered wagon, Gretchen asks her father to let her ride their old mare, Anna. Her father ties her on the horse so she won't fall off. Gretchen falls asleep; and the horse wanders away from the wagon train, following a herd of wild mustangs. When Gretchen awakes, she is in the middle of the Texas plains with no wagons in sight! The white stallion is the leader of the horses and adept at lifting Gretchen off and onto her horse!

I Need to Read an Autobibliography—You Know, a Book about a Person

As the Waltz Was Ending, by Emma Macalik Butterworth. Four Winds, 1982.

Emma Macalik is a ballet student in Vienna when World War II starts. She has already experienced the family's decline in prosperity, and she knows she is no longer a little girl but a very young woman—and talented enough to be a ballerina. Unfortunately, within a year the German troops move in, and St. Stephen's Cathedral is bombed by the British in retaliation for the bombing of the cathedral in Coventry, England. Emma is picked up off the streets, hauled away to cook for Russian soldiers in a farmhouse, and physically abused; but she manages to escape to Vienna.

Bill Peet, an Autobiography, by Bill Peet. Houghton, 1989.

Peet is from Grandview, Indiana. He tells and draws his life story for us. As a child he loved to draw, and he received formal training at an art school after high school. During the Depression when he had a chance to go to the Disney Studios, he hooked a ride to California; and his wife, Margaret, joined him later. He worked as an illustrator for Walt Disney for twenty-seven years, from the making of *Dumbo* to the filming of *Mary Poppins.* He is also a well-known children's book author.

Charlie Brown, Snoopy and Me, by Charles M. Schulz. Doubleday, 1980.

Schulz writes about his career before Peanuts and about how he conceived the comic strip, which began in 1950 with Charlie

Brown and Snoopy. A year later Schroeder was added and the next year, Lucy and Linus. He talks about his feelings toward his creations and about cartooning.

My Life as an Astronaut, by Alan Bean. Pocket Books, 1988.
As a child, Alan Bean's dream was to be a pilot. This dream came true, and he went even further—he walked on the moon and lived on Skylab, our first orbiting space station. Later, he became the first astronaut-artist, painting pictures of the moon and the earth as he saw them from space.

My Life with the Chimpanzees, by Jane Goodall. Pocket Books, 1988.
The well-known naturalist explains why she decided to study animal behavior, telling about her childhood and education. She describes her study of chimpanzees, which she began in Tanzania, Africa, in 1960. Goodall says that once you have been close to chimpanzees, you can tell them apart as easily as you can your classmates.

Nadja, on My Way, by Nadja Salerno-Sonnenberg. Crown, 1989.
The way of a musician is hard; but when music is an overpowering passion, you can do anything! This famous violinist tells the story of her early life humorously and casually, describing periods of both success and self-doubt in a style which includes many sports metaphors. She came to America in 1969 when she was eight years old to study, as she had already shown promise as a musician. In 1981 she won the Naumburg International Prize, and her lifework became clearer to her.

On the Way Home, by Laura Ingalls Wilder. Harper, 1962.
The diary of Laura Ingalls Wilder tells of her family's move from South Dakota to Mansfield, Missouri, from July 17 to August 30, 1894. As they near their destination, they grow to like the country and the people. Her daughter, Rose, who was seven years old at the time, adds some information to the book about the family before and after the journey.

Prairie-Town Boy, by Carl Sandburg. Odyssey, 1990.
The great American poet tells of his boyhood days growing up in the Illinois town of Galesburg. He gives an account of his Swedish ancestry, school days, family life, boyhood jobs, first paydays, life on the road as a hobo, and entrance into the army in 1898.

Self-portrait: Margot Zemach, by Margot Zemach. Addison-Wesley, 1978.

Zemach was born in Hollywood during the years of the Great Depression and went back there for high school. She spent a year in Vienna on a Fulbright Scholarship and met the man she married. They lived in several places in Europe before her husband, Harve, died in 1974. She now lives with her three children in Berkeley, California. We know her as a Caldecott-winning author and illustrator of children's books.

I Want That Book about Things and People with Wings

The Emperor and the Kite, by Jane Yolen. World, 1967.

The emperor's youngest daughter is so small she's often overlooked completely; but when the emperor is captured and imprisoned in a tower, Djeow Seow, using her kite, is the only one who can help him stay alive and escape. After that, he rules with her beside him.

The Fairy Rebel, by Lynne Reid Banks. Doubleday, 1985.

Tiki is a winged fairy about the size and weight of a butterfly. When she is earthed, which happens whenever she touches a human, she becomes visible; and she makes friends with Jan and Charles, who would like to have children. In fact, she becomes the fairy-mother of their daughter Bindi and sends her a series of magical gifts on her birthdays.

Flight of the Moth-Kin, by Kathy Kennedy Tapp. McElderry, 1987.

The Moth-Kin, who are winged like moths, escape but are still in the giants' land. There are three young ones and three older ones: Mother, her daughters Ripple and Lissa, her son Crick, Uncle Kane, and Pan, who will probably marry the children's mother. They would never have made it to their home, the river, without Old Ivy, who was once a Moth-Kin, or without the wings received by the young ones. Ripple is often too enthusiastic in her flight and learns to use her ability only after she gets to know Old Ivy and glimpses the larger world through the wonder of flight.

The Moon Dragon, by Moira Miller. Dial, 1989.

Ling Po is the most boastful young man in China. He readily

accepts the challenge of an old woman of the village to make the finest kite ever seen, one to fly to the moon and carry a man, and decides to call it Moon Dragon. Instead of forgetting about his boast, the people gossip about it; and the news finally reaches the emperor, who decides to come with his court to see Ling Po take off. In the air, Ling Po keeps his eyes shut, doing so until he feels a bump and knows he is landing. He is surprised to arrive in the *new land* but still boastful until he hears laughter and realizes . . . he hasn't gone anywhere! From that day on, all that people have to say is "Ling Po" to make others laugh and forget their cares, for they all know the story.

Peter Pan, by J. M. Barrie. Scribner, 1921.
Neverland is an island off the mainland; and Peter Pan, who wants to remain a boy always, is the leader of the children who live there—some of them lost boys and others who are visitors, such as Wendy and her brothers, John and Michael. Also living there are pirates, redskins, mermaids, fairies, and every kind of beast, so there are numerous battles. Most children arrive there after they have learned to fly, a feat they perform by thinking "lovely wonderful thoughts" that lift them into the air—plus by receiving the help of a fairy, which Peter assumes each child has.

The Silver Pony, a Story in Pictures, by Lynd Ward. Houghton, 1973.
The boy is spanked for holding up work on the farm with his story that he has seen a winged pony in the sky. The next time he sees it, he feeds it an apple and rides it above the countryside and beyond, making friends, distributing fruit and flowers, and helping people or animals in distress. Eventually too close to the center of the cosmos, he and the pony are hurled to earth. His illness is cured when he receives a real pony as a gift.

Thumbelina, by Hans Christian Andersen, retold by Amy Ehrlich. Dial, 1979.
Thumbelina is a tiny little girl who is no larger than a thumb when she is born and who never grows up. She is stolen by a toad but escapes and lives alone during the summer, and the field mice help her stay out of the cold in the winter. She helps a swallow that seems to be dead but recovers from an illness and prevents Thumbelina's approaching marriage to a mole, which will keep her underground. He carries her off and deposits her on a flower, where she finds a winged prince who is just her size.

I'd Like to Read
a Chapter Book

CHAPTER BOOKS

Be a Perfect Person in Just Three Days, by Stephen Manes. Clarion, 1982.

Hit on the head by a book while he is at the library, Milo naturally picks it up and checks it out because the title is—yes, you guessed it—*Be a Perfect Person in Just Three Days*. His father finds the book and promises to keep his lips sealed, as they wait to see what happens on the third, and final, day. Being perfect should be easy if Milo concentrates on all the rewards that will come to a perfect person—such as not having to attend school.

The Beast in Ms. Rooney's Room, by Patricia Reilly Giff. Delacorte, 1984.

After being held back one year in school, Richard Best, alias the Beast, always seems to be in trouble, until he becomes interested in reading and his schoolwork gets easier. His group, led by the reading teacher, Mrs. Paris, wins top honors—eventually; and Richard readies his drawings of each person in the group to put on the bulletin board. When Mrs. Paris looks at them, she uses his real name as a compliment—Best is the best.

Birdy and the Ghosties, by Jill Paton Walsh. Farrar, 1989.

Birdy helps her father, a ferryman, row passengers across the river. When three ghosts want to be towed to an unknown island, her second sight allows her to see and help them. She receives a valuable present, but the understanding she gains of life's fine, rare moments is more valuable.

Cam Jansen and the Mystery of the Gold Coins, by David A. Adler. Viking, 1982.
The camera that Cam is using in her science project disappears from the fair, and she uses her photographic memory to find it. In her search, she discovers that a dealer has been robbed of two gold coins that are more than one hundred years old.

The Case of the Nervous Newsboy, by E. W. Hildick. Macmillan, 1976.
Since they specialize in detective work, Jack McGurk and the members of his club are practicing shadowing people. They become puzzled by the behavior of Simon, the local newsboy—and he becomes puzzled by their behavior, too. When Simon disappears, his mother is worried and reports it to the police. The McGurk Organization, Private Investigators, report what they know to the police and set out to find more information.

The Ghost in Tent 19, by Jim and Jane O'Connor. Random, 1988.
An old treasure map and ghost stories told around the fire lead the campers in tent 19, Danny, Jed, Hal, and Arthur, to expect a ghost—but not really! Danny agrees to be the lookout while the others dig for treasure with spoons from the kitchen, so he is the first one to see the ghost boy, who reappears to all of them and asks them to "keep on digging, please."

Robin Hill, by Carol Greene. Harper, 1986.
When things go wrong, Robin blames Mr. and Mrs. Potts, who own the apartment building where her family lives. She realizes how unfair she is when Mr. Potts rescues her from the roof and Mrs. Potts brings her an orange kitten.

Sarah, Plain and Tall, by Patricia MacLachlan. Harper, 1985.
When their father invites a prospective bride to come live with them in their prairie home, she lets them know she lives by the sea, can sing, has a cat, is tall and plain, and will come for one month. Caleb and Anna are captivated by her and hope she will stay.

Star, by Jo Ann Simon. Random, 1989.
Toni has always felt inferior to her sister Lara, who is slender and graceful, has long blond hair, is a good athlete, and is an honor

student. When she begins to take riding lessons, Toni is sure that she will feel even fatter and more awkward; but to her surprise she feels at home on her horse from the very first and even volunteers to go and help at the stables after school three days a week. She even begins to lose weight. Then she is asked to compete in a beginners' class at a local horse show. Can she possibly do all the things she's learned—with other people watching and with the judges awarding prizes?

What's Cooking, Jenny Archer? by Ellen Conford. Little, 1989.

Jenny is a better cook than she is a businesswoman. The idea is to sell good and attractive lunches to her friends at school; soon she is losing money. She'd better try writing a cookbook!

Wonder Kid Meets the Evil Lunch Snatcher, by Lois Duncan. Little, 1988.

To avoid further lunch snatching, four students create Wonder Kid, a superhero inspired by their favorite comic-book heroes. The resources are a Halloween Superman costume, leftover Fourth of July smoke bombs, and a battery-powered wand from a chemistry set. Will that be enough to scare Matt and his gang?

REAL CHAPTER BOOKS

The Candy Corn Contest, by Patricia Reilly Giff. Yearling, 1984.

Ms. Rooney is holding a Thanksgiving contest. Students in her class are to guess how many candy corns are in the jar, and the winner gets them all. Before he can stop himself, Richard secretly eats three pieces. His worries increase when he forgets to bring an apple the day that the class makes applesauce and when he starts making plans for an upcoming sleep-over.

Horrible Harry and the Green Slime, by Suzy Kline. Viking, 1989.

Doug and Harry are best friends and, at one time, secret pals. One chapter tells how their class celebrates the reading of *Charlotte's Web.* In the final, really funny chapter, the class stages demonstrations, including one where they spike the principal's hair! Harry's teacher, the principal, and the librarian at South School are not afraid of anything horrible. Does that include Harry's green slime?

More Stories Julian Tells, by Ann Cameron. Knopf, 1986.

Inspired by their father's theory that people should not be bored, Julian, his younger brother, Huey, and his best friend, Gloria, seem well able to carry any interesting idea to the point of disaster. Fortunately, their parents are good, and smart in dealing with their kids when some of the children's activities end in disappointment. You will also appreciate Gloria's success in moving the sun, which is not a disaster.

My Robot Buddy, by Alfred Slote. Lippincott, 1975.

Having a robot for a best friend may sound far-fetched now, but Jack doesn't have any friends who live close to his home, and he wants and gets a robot as a tenth-birthday present. It takes a bit of adjustment; Danny, the robot, is programmed especially for Jack—he can't eat with Jack, but he can climb trees with him. When a robot-napper tries to steal Jack's buddy, he has trouble knowing whom or what to steal, as Danny and Jack keep the thief confused until the police arrive.

Nora and Mrs. Mind-Your-Own-Business, by Johanna Hurwitz. Morrow, 1977.

Mrs. Mind-Your-Own-Business has an opinion about everything and everyone, and that's why Nora calls her Mrs. Mind-Your-Own-Business. Life in the apartment house where they all live is seldom dull, from treats and tricks to a power failure and candles. When Nora and her younger brother Teddy learn Mrs. Mind-Your-Own-Business is to be their baby-sitter, they are prepared for the worst and ask her to be a fairy godmother! Happy endings do exist when she learns—and likes—the business of being a fairy godmother.

Oh Paul! by Mary Rayner. Barron's, 1988.

Paul has a hard time. He can't spell very well, and he tends to forget things. "Oh, Paul," he often hears. Even his football-player costume is not what it should be—it doesn't look like one for a character out of a book, like the Heidi costume that Amanda is wearing. However, when a disaster at the costume parade involves Heidi's goat and the famous television star who is judging the contest, Paul saves the day.

The Pizza Pie Slugger, by Jean Marzollo. Random, 1989.

Third-grader Billy plays on the Castle Pizza baseball team. Normally he's a pretty good player, but lately he's been striking out, and he's sure his baby half-sister, Lily, is to blame. Billy's pizza-making grandfather Nonno helps him to build self-confidence and overcome his negative feelings. Billy learns a lot more from his grandfather than just how to make pizza-moon pizza.

I Want a Book about Boys and Girls

And You Give Me a Pain, Elaine, by Stella Pevsner. Seabury, 1978.

Andrea's older sister Elaine keeps ruining Andrea's home-side plans with her wild and dramatic antics, which are offset by Joe, an older brother, who understands Andrea's problem. If things would just calm down, Andrea might have a chance with Chris and better grades. Her school-side life includes Robyn, her best friend, and Robyn's advice column, on which they both work.

The Cybil War, by Betsy Byars. Viking, 1981.

Simon and Tony are both in love with the same girl, Cybil Ackerman. When Tony tries to sabotage Simon's chances with Cybil, the war is on! Tony sets up the movies for four, and after the movies Harriet tells Simon the truth—Cybil thought she was going with Simon! When Simon and Cybil ride their bicycles past Tony's house that evening, Simon feels assured the war is over, because Cybil prefers him.

In Trouble Again, Zelda Hammersmith? by Lynn Hall. Harcourt, 1987.

Zelda has trouble convincing a boy that he is indeed her new boyfriend—her first love-life trouble. In fact, he never really has much chance to enter her life, because she has to take care of an "F" in arithmetic, plot to foil a bully, get a birthday gift that her mother wants (but would have preferred live), and overcome the loss of her best friend, which happens in the summer—the worst time.

The Josie Gambit, by Mary Francis Shura. Dodd, 1986.

Beautiful Tory Mitchell plays a high-risk game with her family and her friend Josie Nolan, who is twelve and the only one who has ever beaten Greg Farrell three times straight at chess. (It was Josie's grandfather who had taught Josie and Greg to play chess.) It is Greg, who is twelve also and a neighbor, staying again at his grandmother's, who recognizes Tory's gambit and calls her bluff, even though it will hurt Josie and Tory's father.

Julia's Mending, by Kathy Lynn Emerson. Orchard, 1987.

Upon her arrival at her aunt's and uncle's farm on July 22, 1887, Julia records in her journal that the children are beastly. Simon is the oldest, followed by twin boys, two very young girls, and Grace, who is nearest to Julia in age and with whom Julia must share a bed. The next day, Julia falls through the hay hole in the barn and spends several very unhappy weeks in bed with a broken leg. She has no other choice: Her missionary parents are in China and her grandmama has left New York City for Europe. A one-room schoolhouse with fourteen students is also a disappointment, and she suspects that someone has taken her journal to read.

Rosy's Romance, by Sheila Greenwald. Little, 1989.

Rosy and Hermione dream up Project Romance to help Rosy's teenage sisters with their love lives—not that her sisters need or want this help. Anitra and Pippa wear outfits (prom clothes, circa 1956, from the Lomax Thrift Shop) that have been assembled for them as a joke on their boyfriends, Pete and JoJo, who decided to do the same thing. Project Romance is explained, and they leave for their prom. Little does Rosy know how Project Romance will really turn out for her as she leaves for *her* school party in a new dress (a wallflower dress from the preteen department).

Sixth-Grade Sleepover, by Eve Bunting. Harcourt, 1986.

When the Rabbit Reading Club plans a sleepover at school, Janey is afraid to go to it because the other Rabbits will discover her embarrassing problem. With help from her parents and best friend Claudia, she finds the courage to go, even though Blake Conway will be there and see her in her pajamas! During the evening she wonders why both Pebbles, the real rabbit, and Rosie Green, the new girl, are acting strangely. Do they have problems as embarrassing as her own?

Standing Out, by Jamie Suzanne, created by Francine Pascal. Bantam, 1988.

Billie, or Belinda, is Sweet Valley's best pitcher and has plenty of friends; but her closest ones are Jim, the team's catcher, and the twins, Elizabeth and Jessica. She feels very close to her father because of her athletic ability and especially now that her mother is pregnant. When Billie's menstrual period starts for the first time, she has more worries than she anticipated but more luck and assistance in coping with events than she expected. Fortunately, the game in which she is pitching badly is rained out, and she will have another chance. The twins see to it that she appears at a birthday party looking like a girl, which surprises but pleases Jim. When she holds the new baby, she knows she is growing up and happy with the changes that had seemed awful the week before.

Taffy Sinclair and the Secret Admirer Epidemic, by Betsy Haynes. Bantam, 1988.

If her girlfriends all have dates for the movie on Saturday with boys who are Randy's friends, why hasn't he asked her? Jana is pretty concerned, because Taffy Sinclair is flirting with Randy, but a typewritten note signed "Secret Admirer," found in her desk drawer, distracts her. There are more notes to her—and to others. Finally, a faint suspicion becomes strong enough for Jana to make plans that will outsmart Taffy and resolve the affair to her satisfaction, a date with Randy.

I Like Books That . . .

MAKE ME HAPPY AND SAD

Bridge to Terabithia, by Katherine Paterson. Harper, 1977.
> Jess and Leslie begin as rivals at school and end up as wonderful friends. They turn a spot in the woods into Terabithia, an imaginary kingdom, where they can escape their problems and dream. They are helping each other grow, and then tragedy strikes.

Charlotte's Web, by E. B. White. Harper, 1952.
> Wilbur, the runt pig, should have been killed, but Fern rescues him; and the animals in the barnyard comfort him at Zuckerman's farm. These friends include Templeton the rat; but it is ultimately Charlotte, the spider, who saves Wilbur from being butchered with her remarkable web writing.

The Doll in the Garden, a Ghostly Story, by Mary Downing Hahn. Clarion, 1989.
> When Ashley and her friend Kristi visit with Louisa, who died seventy years ago at the age of nine, and also find a doll in Miss Cooper's garden, Miss Cooper is very upset with them; but she is finally reconciled to her own actions and tells them about the time when she knew Louisa. Like Miss Cooper, Ashley begins to understand her own feelings about the recent death of her father.

The Endless Steppe: Growing Up in Siberia, by Esther Hautzig. Crowell, 1968.
> Esther and her family are relatively happy with their life, even though they are barely surviving in Russian-occupied Vilna, Poland, in 1941. Then they are arrested and shipped to Siberia. Esther's

father is separated from them, and they all must endure the winters on the treeless plain. Through the years they not only hope that they will survive but also that they will see one another again.

Prairie Songs, by Pam Conrad. Harper, 1985.

Dr. Berryman and his wife come from New York, and the Downings welcome them to the Nebraska prairie, teach them needed skills, and share the beauties of the land. Louise and Lester Downing especially appreciate and respond to Emmeline Berryman, who is, however, unable to endure pioneer life.

Roll of Thunder, Hear My Cry, by Mildred D. Taylor. Dial, 1976.

The Logans are a loving family, strong black landholders in Mississippi. They struggle to keep their land and retain their pride and freedom. Cassie Logan tells of their joys and pains in the 1930s.

Sarah, Plain and Tall, by Patricia MacLachlan. Harper, 1985.

To provide for his motherless family living on the prairie, Papa advertises for a wife and mother. Sarah, who lives in Maine, answers; Caleb, Anna, and Papa write to her, and she comes to live with them but misses Maine and the ocean. The children are afraid that when she learns to drive the wagon, she *may* leave them.

Slake's Limbo, by Felice Holman. Scribner, 1974.

Aremis Slake, thirteen years old, survives nearly four months living underground. He decorates a forgotten niche in the wall of a tunnel, retrieves newspapers to resell, eats sparingly at a cafe, and rides the subway trains for pleasure. It is lonely, but he has to hide. His tunnel is more secure than anything he has ever known—until an accident on the tracks focuses attention on his "home" and destroys it. Delirious from depression and hunger, he signals a passing train, which stops in time to save his life. He is hospitalized and forced to deal with luxury and friends; but he has once seen the blue sky and now knows he still wants to be independent and to be up, not down, in every sense of the word.

A Summer to Die, by Lois Lowry. Houghton, 1977.

Molly is beautiful and knows what she wants from life; her sister Meg, who is two years younger, lives with the uncertainty of what she wants to be and is convinced she is not beautiful. That winter the family moves to the country, to a peaceful place where their father can finish his book. In addition to the four in Meg's family, there are Ben and Maria, the other renters, and Will, who owns the properties. Meg is present when Ben and Maria's baby is born, but she is the last to find out about the seriousness of Molly's illness. Both experiences provide the insights into life and death that Meg needs.

Tuck Everlasting, by Natalie Babbitt. Farrar, 1975.

Just think about what you would do if you had the chance to live forever! The Tucks know. Ten-year-old Winnie gets to know the Tucks and their circumstances, and she ponders the blessing and curse of life-everlasting in this world. She has no idea that she has been followed to their home by a stranger with evil intentions. This dilemma forces her to make some very serious decisions about drinking the water that bestows everlasting life.

PLAY WITH WORDS

Amelia Bedelia, by Peggy Parish. Harper, 1963.

Amelia Bedelia will amuse you as she takes everything as it is written—from "drawing the drapes" to "dusting the furniture." Think about the meaning of the last phrase: What kind of dust would you use? However, she bakes a great pie and endears herself to her employers.

CDB, by William Steig. Simon, 1968.

Amusing illustrations depict the phrases created by mostly ingenious letter combinations, which are fun to decode by sounding out the letters and looking at the pictures. I N O. Get it?

How Ships Play Cards: A Beginning Book of Homonyms, by Cynthia Basil. Morrow, 1980.

Homonym comes from a Greek word meaning "same name." Homonyms are the basis for many riddles, because they are words that may be the same in spelling and pronunciation but not in meaning: plant, jam, and bulb, for example. This book explains the development of the double meanings of the words. There is also a lovely little thought with the answer to the riddle of how the ocean says good-bye to a ship.

Mad as a Wet Hen! by Marvin Terban. Clarion, 1987.

Idioms are phrases with hidden meanings; that is, they do not mean exactly what the words say. This book contains more than one hundred common English idioms, many of them humorous. They are organized by category, on subjects such as animals, body parts, feelings, food, hats, and colors. You will "laugh your head off" (to quote one well-known idiom).

Many Luscious Lollipops, a Book about Adjectives, by Ruth Heller. Grosset, 1989.
Luscious and lovely illustrations and a rhymed text describe how adjectives are used and how they can make any story more interesting. Different kinds of adjectives and how to use them are noted, as well as exceptions to the rules. Some information on punctuation and capitalization is included, and you'll meet your old friends—the articles *a, an,* and *the*—plus predicate adjectives, demonstratives, possessives, and proper adjectives.

Murfles and Wink-a-peeps: Funny Old Words for Kids, by Susan Ketz Sperling. Potter, 1985.
Poems and rounds include and describe once-popular old English words, such as *murfles* (freckles) and *wink-a-peeps* (eyes) or *boonfellows, teenful,* and *ha-ha.* Some of the words on the list "Names to Call People" could still be useful today.

Teapot, Switcheroo, and Other Silly Word Games, by Ruthven Tremain. Greenwillow, 1979.
How did *teapot* get into this book and why is a palindrome a sort of switcheroo? Several suggestions of ways to scramble and unscramble letters to make words will get you into the practice of seeing and hearing other possibilities.

Where Are the
Books about . . .

BALLET DANCERS

Battle of the Bunheads, by Jahnna N. Malcolm. Scholastic, 1989.

At the Academy five fledgling ballet dancers on one side and three more-advanced students on the other are in the battle (competition)—the competition to see which student will present flowers to a world-famous ballerina after her performance. Everyone believes that the best dancer in the more-advanced group, Courtney, will easily win. Not so. The guest ballerina has something to say about it, and she picks Mary from the other group. Mary rises to the occasion on the evening of the performance.

Cynthia Gregory Dances Swan Lake, by Cynthia Gregory. Simon, 1990.

Words and colored photographs take you through a day with Cynthia Gregory, star of the American Ballet Theater, as she prepares for and dances the leading role in *Swan Lake.* You'll find out about her family, the classes she takes, what goes on at rehearsal, how she puts on stage makeup, her thoughts while dancing, and how she meets her fans.

Drina Dances Again, by Jean Estoril. Scholastic, 1960.

Both acting and dancing seem to come easily to Drina; and although she is the daughter of a well-known ballerina who was killed in an accident, she wants to make it on the strength of her own abilities and hides her identity. Ballet is her first love, and she is chosen over others at the school to dance small solo parts when she is fourteen. It is exciting, but it only makes her aware that when she faces the critics, people will eventually realize who her mother was. She has some stage fright and fear of failure, but she does what every other performer of note must do—she practices and travels.

Going to My Ballet Class, by Susan Kuklin. Bradbury, 1989.
Jamie has fun at her ballet class. Follow her and the other members of her class through a year of warm-ups, musical beats, right-and-left, steps, positions, and leaps, taking you from floor work to the final bow.

Silent Dancer, by Bruce Hlibok. Messner, 1981.
Training to be a ballet dancer is difficult. Imagine how much harder it would be if you could not hear the music! *Silent Dancer* lets you enter the world of a ten-year-old deaf girl studying ballet at the Joffrey Ballet School.

SPACESHIPS AND STUFF

Commander Toad and the Planet of the Grapes, by Jane Yolen. Coward, 1982.
Before Commander Toad lands their spaceship on a seemingly peaceful planet, he and Lieutenant Lily take the sky skimmer down to investigate; and they find themselves in danger of being swallowed by giant grapes. Lt. Lily escapes and returns to *Star Warts* to get help from the crew. It's all due to allergies, the doctor says; and Commander Toad thinks of jokes that are the grapest.

Guys from Space, by Daniel Pinkwater. Macmillan, 1989.
Getting his mom's absent-minded permission to go off in a spaceship for the day, our hero departs with his dog's water dish, which he wears on his head as a space helmet. The space guys take him to a planet where rocks talk and their plastic fish are acceptable as money. Having root beers with ice cream is so interesting to the space guys, he wonders if they will take him home before they go home to tell everyone about it.

The Iron Giant, a Story in Five Nights, by Ted Hughes. Harper, 1968.
An iron giant who eats anything made of metal agrees to face a space being in a test of strength. Is the space being a bat, an angel, a lizard, or a dragon? It lands in Australia and is so large that its chin sinks into the Indian Ocean. The future of the earth hangs in the

balance! However, these two awful creatures turn out to be peaceful influences.

Piloted Space Flights, by Isaac Asimov. Gareth Stevens, 1990.

Ten flights and the records of their missions are the main topics covered in a period extending from World War II to the present. The rest of the book deals with the selection and training of crews and speculates on what flights will be made in the future—by whom and to where.

When the Tripods Came, by John Christopher. Dutton, 1988.

Laurie sees the tripod descend from space; he sees its destructiveness and watches the fighter-bombers destroy it. It is the first evidence of an alien force, which begins to brainwash the world. Censorship encourages the spread of rumors: Was it a second or third invasion? Did it occur in the USA or France? Will the world ever be free of the threat? Laurie and his family are determined to fight.

The Wonderful Flight to the Mushroom Planet, by Eleanor Cameron. Little, 1954.

In response to a want ad from Mr. Tyco M. Bass, David and Chuck build a spaceship in just three days. Then they are off, with a mascot and a canning jar, where they put the air from Basidium for Mr. Bass. They meet and help the Mushroom people, and their arrival home is wonderful—at first. Then they seem to lose Mr. Bass, a valuable necklace, the spaceship, and the planet—you will understand how it all happens.

SUMMER VACATIONS

Camp Ghost-Away, by Judy Delton. Dell, 1988.

On Friday, Troop 23 boards the bus for Camp Hide-Away, the Pee-Wee Scout camp. During the first night they hear the OOOOOOooooooo of a "ghost," which turns out to be Roger and Sonny; from then on, the camp has a new name. Although on Saturday Molly doesn't do well in learning to float or row a boat and gets poison ivy, on Sunday morning she realizes she is the only one who didn't cry that night from homesickness. Molly doesn't expect any badges and is surprised on Tuesday when the presentations are made.

Eight Mules from Monterey, by Patricia Beatty. Morrow, 1982.

Fayette would like to spend a summer vacation the way the two rich girls with whom she walks home from school spend theirs. However, after the local librarian has an unfortunate accident, Fayette and her brother go with their mother on a mule trip to leave books in homes—the nearest thing to library service in the California mountains in 1916. The summer turns out to be unforgettable, starting with zigzagging up mountains that seem to go straight up.

The Great Skinner Getaway, by Stephanie S. Tolan. Four Winds, 1987.

Summer vacation is going to last more than two weeks for the Skinners; this time, it is going to last all summer. All six of them are to go on a trip in a thirty-five-foot motor home. Those are the plans for which they prepare; but the Skinners always have mishaps, and this vacation is no different. One example of their interesting experiences is their dad's choice to visit Orville Corners on a country road because it doesn't have any tourist attractions. They find, however, that it does have a sheriff!

The Hot and Cold Summer, by Johanna Hurwitz. Morrow, 1984.

Rory and Derek are really looking forward to summer vacation—swimming, riding bikes, reading comics—all the things they like to do together. They don't expect to have to include Bolivia, who is also ten and has come to spend the summer with her aunt. The boys vow to ignore her; but when Derek goes away to camp, Rory finds that unless he makes friends with Bolivia, he is going to have a very lonely, boring vacation.

Just for the Summer, by Christine McDonnell. Viking, 1987.

Her aunts are glad Lydia is spending her vacation with them and her friends, Ivy and Emily. She learns to swim, enters a crafts project in the August fair, and organizes a preschool play group. All throughout the weeks of fun and learning, Lydia also spends a lot of time thinking about, and writing to, her father, who is recovering from a serious illness in a hospital back home.

Lost Boys Never Say Die, by Alan Brown and Grant Forsberg. Delacorte, 1989.

Lewis is supposed to be at Camp Chicopee, which has speech therapists who can help him with his stuttering. However, he jumps off the camp train and goes back to stay in his own home. His parents are far away—at the Arctic Circle. He isn't expecting a strange boy named Max, who moves in; a role in *Peter Pan;* and a really bad stomachache from eating Superdogs.

Stringbean's Trip to the Shining Sea, by Vera B. Williams and Jennifer Williams. Greenwillow, 1988.
   Stringbean and his older brother Fred are spending their vacation traveling to the Pacific Ocean in Fred's truck, which has a small kitchen and a sleeping area in the back. They send many postcards and pictures home to their family to tell of their adventures, which include seeing bears, visiting mines, and trying to catch up with a circus.

The Summer House Cat, by Michele Granger. Dutton, 1989.
   While vacationing on an island with her parents, Charlotte finds a cat, whom she names Little Orphan Annie. Charlotte is determined not to leave for home without Annie, but how is she going to persuade her father to let her keep it? They already have a cat; but fathers can be outvoted in families. It's still a mad scramble as they are leaving, because Annie doesn't show up on time!

Summer Switch, by Mary Rodgers. Harper, 1982.
   While waiting for the bus in New York City that will take him to summer camp, Ben "Ape Face" Andrews wishes he were his father—at the exact same moment his father thinks casually he would like to be in his son's shoes. Suddenly it happens. Ape Face (in his father's body) must go to Beverly Hills, California, to conduct business while his father (trapped inside Ape Face) goes to Camp Soonawissakit. Given his father's occupation and a teacher's request to write about a summer vacation, you may guess the outcome—but not how it comes about.

TRAINS

Aboard a Steam Locomotive, by Huck Scarry. Prentice-Hall, 1987.
   Very few steam locomotives exist today outside of museums, but the era of the 1800s is captured in this book, with sketches of English, American, German, and Swiss trains. The drawings show the parts and types of steam locomotives and how they worked, as well as what people did on the trains and in the sheds to keep them running.

The Big Book of Real Trains, by Walter Retan. Grosset, 1987.

    A brief look at the history of railroading is followed by a close-up that explores the workings of electric and diesel trains of today. Included are the freight and passenger trains and their crews, the famous Japanese and French trains, and, finally, you on a trip with your parents.

The First Train, by Cyriel Verleyen. Crowell, 1968.

    In England a reporter, Samuel Smith, saw Trevithick's first horseless steam wagon in 1801. Later he saw similar vehicles built by George Stephenson to tow several carts and, in 1830, to haul passengers from Liverpool to Manchester. He liked the idea behind this new method of transportation and was very happy for Stephenson, who had become his friend and confidant.

The Iron Road, by Richard Snow. Four Winds, 1978.

    When American railroading began with the construction of the Baltimore and Ohio railroad in 1827, wooden rails were very dangerous, and accidents were frequent. Steel rails, the Civil War, the westward movement, hoboes, and strikers were all important to the development of railroads, as they moved into the 1900s with lots of freight to haul. The story of Casey Jones and the diesel engine kept railroading alive until the recent midcentury decline. The train still has a magic about it and is being looked at again as a feasible means of transportation.

A Regularly Rolling Noah, by George Ella Lyon. Bradbury, 1986.

    Taking care of farm animals in a boxcar is a new experience for the boy from Pathfork, Kentucky, hired to tend to the cow and her calf, chickens, a horse, a goat, and a pig that the Creech family is moving by train to Canada.

Train Talk, an Illustrated Guide to Lights, Hand Signals, Whistles, and Other Language of Railroading, by Roger Yepsen. Pantheon, 1983.

    Trains and the people who run them communicate in many very complicated and fascinating ways. Remember, a train engineer doesn't have a steering wheel to use to avoid hitting something, so he must rely on sounds and lights and various other signaling devices.

The Train to Grandma's, by Ivan Gantschev. Picture Book Studio, 1987.

Jeff and Marina's journey to visit their grandparents is by train and boat. It is the first time they have gone alone, but they are not sad or scared. The train races *through* the pages of the book—literally; and just before they get on the boat, their dog Rufus appears and gets on with them.

I Want an Adventure Story about a Modern Child Which Is Not a Mystery or a Fantasy or a Ghost Story or a Science Fiction Story or a War Story or Anything to Do with Sports

Hooples on the Highway, by Stephen Manes. Coward, 1978.

When Alvin and his family take a trip to Philadelphia, the Hooples are looking forward to the excitement of being there and are unprepared for all the mishaps along the way, like Sadie's misadventure with a tractor trailer and a CB; mosquitoes; or a somewhat unfortunate night in a small-town motel. Being a day late for bat night at the baseball game turns out okay after all, or so *they think.*

The Kidnapping of Courtney Van Allen and What's-Her-Name, by Joyce Cool. Knopf, 1981.

When a very famous twelve-year-old is kidnapped, Jan Travis, who's visiting her aunt in New York City, is accidentally kidnapped at the same time. Jan and Courtney strike up an uneasy friendship on the remote island where they watch the kidnapper's old movies. Try to escape? Of course they will. And they will also try to find out why Courtney was grabbed.

Lost in the Devil's Desert, by Gloria Skurzynski. Lothrop, 1982.

The family stops to see Gram in a small town in Utah, and the next morning two men steal a truck without knowing Kevin is in the back. He escapes—only to discover the total emptiness of the desert. Survival lore, a determination to see his dad again before his father's departure for military duty, and two lucky breaks get him to the hospital in time to save his life.

Night of the Twisters, by Ivy Ruckman. Crowell, 1984.

When a tornado destroys their entire neighborhood, twelve-year-old Dan and his friend Arthur must save themselves and Dan's baby brother. This is based on a real event—a series of tornadoes on June 4, 1980, in Grand Junction, Nebraska.

Shadow Shark, by Colin Thiele. Harper, 1985.

Joe and his cousin Meg are stranded with Meg's father on a deserted island after their boat explodes during a hunt for Scarface, a great white shark, off the coast of Australia. Meg's father is badly hurt when the boat goes down, Joe's dog dies, and they are soon tired of eating fish and very hungry when rescued.

The Talking Earth, by Jean Craighead George. Harper, 1983.

Billie Wind, a Seminole Indian girl, is told to take a dugout into the Florida Everglades as punishment for doubting the spirits that live there. During her days alone, she survives a fire and a brutal storm and returns with ideas about uniting the old beliefs of her people with scientific knowledge to save the land.

Voyage of the Frog, by Gary Paulsen. Orchard, 1989.

His uncle taught him to sail; and when his uncle dies, he leaves his sailboat the *Frog* to David, who is fourteen years old, to use to scatter his ashes at sea off the southern California coast. Afterward, David is blown off course by a windstorm. The boat looks like a garbage scow after the storm, and David has head and shoulder pains; but he and the boat make it to the mid-Baja area, where there is a chance of picking up David but not the *Frog*. It has been nine days, but after receiving a gift of food from the passing boat, he and the *Frog* continue to sail northward.

Do You Have Any Make-Believe Books?

Bailey's Window, by Anne Lindbergh. Harcourt, 1984.

Carl and Anna Carlson and their dog, Leif the Lucky, live in the country with their parents, and they are as eager as their new neighbor Ingrid is for her to become a Viking Club member. She renames her dog Eric the Red before her grandmother, with whom she is staying, can say his name is Squirrel! Carl and Anna think their cousin from New York City, Bailey Bond, is a pain in the neck; and he has to earn his way into the club after he arrives for the summer. However, he draws pictures of windows that he can actually climb through; and they discover that they can all get involved in the scenes, which have come alive. They also discover that Bailey is really just very unhappy over his lost dog. Do you know how they found the dog and how they could have done it more quickly?

The Book of Three, by Lloyd Alexander. Dell, 1964.

Prydain is a country of the imagination where the assistant pigkeeper Taran and the princess Eilonwy live. Taran departs with his assorted companions to fight against Arawan's powers of darkness for Prince Gwydion, in this story from Welsh mythology.

Elidor, by Alan Garner. Walck, 1965.

Four children, three brothers and their sister, start out to find Thursday Street, after Roland, who is intrigued with the mechanical street map of Manchester, suggests it must surely be an interesting place with a name like that. They find themselves transported to the mysterious Kingdom of Elidor, where they become involved in a dangerous struggle with the strange and terrible forces of darkness.

They return with the responsibility of the Treasures, which mysteriously possess static electricity. Findhorn, a unicorn, could have saved Elidor for the four of them with his song, but they are left alone in the slum.

The Fairy Rebel, by Lynne Reid Banks. Doubleday, 1985.

When Tiki, a young fairy, uses her magic on humans, she knows it may mean her own death. After using up her own, she borrows so much magic for Jan and Charles that she asks them to name their baby Bindi, which means "expensive." Although they do not see Tiki after that, they know and appreciate the unique birthday gifts that Bindi receives each year until she is eight.

Gom on Windy Mountain, by Grace Chetwin. Lothrop, 1986.

Gom is the tenth child and ten years old when he begins to know he is a bit unusual. He enters the world of wizardry and magic, as he follows the call of a mysterious stone rune left to him by his mother. After his father dies, Gom considers very seriously the difference between belonging on the mountain and going Far Away, "over there" somewhere.

The Hobbit, by J. R. R. Tolkien. Houghton, 1984.

Persuaded by the wizard Gandalf, Bilbo Baggins (a hobbit) sets off with a band of dwarfs to capture the treasure stolen by Smaug the Dragon. Small even by dwarf standards, Bilbo proves his value through pluck, luck, and the help of a magical ring.

Jumanji, by Chris Van Allsburg. Houghton, 1981.

When Judy's and Peter's parents leave them home alone for the evening, the children decide to play with a safari game they find in the park. At first it seems like just another boring board game, but then Peter's first move lands him on a square on which is written "lion attack," and a *real* lion appears on top of the piano! Next, Judy's move produces two monkeys who tear the kitchen apart. One disaster follows another—but they can't stop playing until one of them reaches the golden city of Jumanji.

The Magic Grandfather, by Jay Williams. Four Winds, 1979.

Each generation in the town since before the American Revolution has had a Limner family, and each Limner family has had a magician. Sam finds out accidentally that his grandfather is a magician—perhaps the last one in the family, since neither he nor his father has the talent. The possibility of becoming a magician amazes him but does not take hold of him as a real interest until he distracts his grandfather in a demonstration and his grandfather is transported through the portal to another place called Beta and doesn't return. Sam asks Sarah, his cousin, to help him, as he tries to learn quickly from his grandfather's books how to cast spells and summon people so he can get his grandfather home.

Mighty Magic, by Selden M. Loring. Holiday, 1937.

Granny Matten and Jack Hollis enjoy each other's company, and she gives him an old Indian drum when she must move because she owes the bank money. He doesn't know that it really can call up Indians or that the chief's whistle can bring out pirates, but he is sharp enough to ask them if any treasure is buried nearby! Guess what? There is.

The Snow Spider, by Jenny Nimmo. Dutton, 1986.

One of five strange gifts from his grandmother on Gwyn's tenth birthday is a yellow scarf that belonged to his sister Bethan, who disappeared four years ago. The gifts confer on him the power of an ancient magician, and he confides some of this to Eirlys, an orphan. Her presence has healed the family's sorrow over the loss of Bethan and her departure signals that he must choose the kind of life he wishes for himself.

Treehorn's Treasure, by Florence Parry Heide. Holiday, 1981.

Treehorn places an envelope, which is addressed to "Instant Magic," with a dollar bill and a coupon enclosed, into the hole of the maple tree, because his father says Treehorn must learn to save money. He then discovers that the tree has dollar bills for leaves. Although he tells this to people, they do not believe him. He is glad that he picked a few of the leaves and spent the money for new comic books and candy, because the next day his father wants to start a savings account for him with the dollar. He is sorry that the ripe dollar bills fade on the branches after he has to remove the envelope.

Winter of Magic's Return, by Pamela F. Service. Atheneum, 1985.

Earl, Heather, and Welly (Wellington)—an orphan, an un-wanted child, and a boy who wants to go to a military school—are at the best school in Wales and becoming friends when the appearance of Earl's fake relatives makes escape necessary. A fall brings Earl's lost memory back, and Heather and Welly go with Earl (who is really Merlin) in search of King Arthur, although it has been two thousand years since King Arthur ruled. They have to fight evil magic to reach Avalon and convince King Arthur he should return, because England is now in a state of devastation in which both roses and unicorns are probably extinct.

I Have to Read a
Biography at Least
150 Pages Long

America's Mark Twain, by May McNeer. Houghton, 1962.

Little Sam, Sammy, Sam—all were used as nicknames by Samuel (his real name) up to page 76 in this book. When he started writing funny stories, he used the name Mark Twain. Honored by Oxford University, he liked his book about Joan of Arc the best, but his greatest books, *Tom Sawyer, Huckleberry Finn,* and *Life on the Mississippi,* are thoroughly American.

Amos Fortune, Free Man, by Elizabeth Yates. Dutton, 1950.

Born a prince in his African tribe, Amos Fortune was kidnapped in 1725 by slavers and forced to bear inhuman conditions in a slave ship. He was lucky enough, however, to be bought by a kindly Boston Quaker family and later learned to be a leather tanner and bought his freedom. Through careful saving he was able to buy freedom for several other slaves and eventually became a highly respected citizen and benefactor of Jaffrey, New Hampshire, where he and his wife are buried.

The Endless Steppe: Growing Up in Siberia, by Esther Hautzig. Crowell, 1968.

Esther was only ten years old when Russian soldiers arrested her family and sent them to Siberia as laborers for being Polish, Jewish, and capitalists. At first, life was as monotonous as the landscape; and the pleasures of food, a light at night, school, and companions her age—even the beauty of the first snow—seemed better than they were. She said good-bye to the unique beauty of the steppe in 1946 at the age of fifteen when she returned to Vilna.

Sojourner Truth and the Struggle for Freedom, by Edward Beecher
  Claflin. Barron's, 1987.

Born into slavery, young Belle escaped to New York City where
she became Sojourner Truth, speaking out against slavery before
and after the Civil War. She took this new name in 1843 when
she started her preaching mission, moving about the country and
listened to eagerly by audiences. In 1870 her goal became the secur-
ing of signatures on a petition to grant land to freed slaves.

Traitor: The Case of Benedict Arnold, by Jean Fritz. Putnam, 1981.

Mystery surrounds one of America's smartest generals during
the Revolutionary War, and he became hated as a traitor after the
war. "Incredible" is the only word that describes his personal duels,
business deals, and leadership of the Americans throughout a good
deal of wilderness fighting. From his viewpoint, he upheld his
honor, defending it against any slight; yet he planned to give the
British the control of the Hudson River when he asked for, and
received, the command of West Point under the new title of Major
General Arnold, a post conferred on him by General George Washington. He escaped a traitor's death but not his guilt.

The Upstairs Room, by Johanna Reiss. Crowell, 1972.

Afraid of being sent to a Jewish concentration camp, ten-year-
old Annie and her big sister Sini hid from the Germans for more
than two years, staying with a farm family in Holland during World
War II. Her departure from the house—free again, able to see Canadian soldiers go by along the main road—was followed a month later
by a reunion with her family. Later in life she moved to the United
States; but she eventually returned to show her daughters her room,
which was kept intact.

I Want an Adventure Story Where the People Survive Danger

The Cay, by Theodore Taylor. Doubleday, 1969.

Living on a Dutch island off the coast of Venezuela, Phillip has never felt comfortable with black people; but all that changes—must change—when he wakes up on a raft after their evacuation boat is torpedoed by the Nazis. Phillip finds himself with an old black man named Timothy and the ship's scrawny cat, and on the second day, Phillip goes blind.

The Goats, by Brock Cole. Collins, 1987.

You often hear the expression "Kids can be cruel." How cruel? Cruel enough to strip a boy and a girl of their clothes and leave them all alone at night on an island. Laura and Howie, the most unpopular and nerdy kids at the summer camp, survive this ordeal and even triumph.

Hatchet, by Gary Paulsen. Bradbury, 1987.

Alone in the Canadian wilderness! After the pilot of the small plane he is riding in dies of a heart attack, Brian survives the inevitable crash. However, now he is totally lost and hundreds of miles from civilization, with only his wits and a hatchet to keep him alive.

My Side of the Mountain, by Jean George. Dutton, 1959.

Leaving a small New York City apartment, fourteen-year-old Sam Gribley dreams of finding the old Gribley farm and living independently in the mountains. He makes that dream come true with a minimum of equipment, such as flint and steel and some knowledge of outdoor living, such as how to boil water in a leaf. He also has the assistance of friendly humans, a librarian for one, and of animals, such as Frightful, a falcon. Of course, it isn't easy!

Save Queen of Sheba, by Louise Moeri. Dutton, 1981.

Queen of Sheba, King David—funny-sounding names to us today; but back in the days of the wagon trains, names from the Bible were more common. It isn't every day, though, that a twelve-year-old boy, King David, wakes up after an Indian attack to find himself half scalped and all alone except for his little sister, Queen of Sheba, whom he must care for until they *may* possibly find their parents alive in the wagons ahead, *if* any escaped this attack.

The Sign of the Beaver, by Elizabeth George Speare. Houghton, 1983.

In 1769, twelve-year-old Matt is left alone in the family's new cabin in the Maine woods while his father goes back to Massachusetts to pick up Matt's mother, sister, and the new baby. Neither Matt nor his father realizes how long the journey will take or foresees the hardships and challenges Matt will face. With the help of Attean, an Indian boy, Matt learns the age-old skills he needs to live off the land and finds companionship in the long, lonely months.

Do You Have Any Books Where the Toys Come Alive?

Among the Dolls, by William Sleator. Dutton, 1975.

A little girl receives the unwanted gift of a dollhouse and its doll family and treats them carelessly and meanly. To her horror, she shrinks to their size and receives the same unkindness from them. Her return to real size seems impossible, even with the help of Dandaroo, the youngest doll.

The Bears' House, by Marilyn Sachs. Doubleday, 1971.

Ill-treated and ignored by her classmates and neglected by her emotionally disturbed mother, Fran Ellen finds comfort in playing with a dollhouse and its occupants—three toy bears who come to life for her. The Bears' House was made for Ellen's teacher, who will retire soon, and she intends to give it to someone in the class. Nobody is happy when Fran Ellen wins it, but the teacher knows Fran Ellen has earned it through fulfilling real-life family responsibilities.

The Indian in the Cupboard, by Lynne Reid Banks. Doubleday, 1980.

When Omri combines two ordinary birthday presents—a plastic Indian and an old cabinet for which he finds a key—he becomes host and protector to a live but miniature Indian brave, Little Bear, who wants company and gets it—a cowboy and an Indian girl.

The Phantom Tollbooth, by Norman Juster. Random, 1961.

Milo, bored with school and life, finds two gifts—a toy car and a real turnpike tollbooth, complete with tokens and map—in his room. He drives through the tollbooth and finds himself in a land of words and double meanings. He meets Tock, the watchdog, who accompanies him in the car that moves as long as Milo thinks. After many interesting events, the tollbooth is a welcome sight; but it is gone the next day, leaving him to wonder if he would have had time for another trip, since there is so much to do now at home.

The Teddy Bear Tree, by Barbara Dillon. Morrow, 1982.

In the place where she buried the glass eye of an old, stuffed bear, Bertine discovers that a tree has grown overnight. The tree's fruit is unusual: Hanging from its limbs are teddy bears! She has ten bears, and she finds that Joel can walk—and talk—to humans. He also turns out to be pretty bossy.

When the Dolls Woke, by Marjorie Filley Stover. Whitman, 1985.

The dolls have known several generations of the Wurling family, and they know Aunt Abby, who is nearly ninety, needs money now—not later when her house in Boston sells. The dolls think hard to communicate the place of the hidden treasure—even loosening the stone in the dollhouse's fireplace. Will Gail, who has inherited the dollhouse, and her aunt understand the clues that have been left by the former owners and by the dolls?

How Do You Draw Things?

Draw 50 Monsters, Creeps, Superheroes, Demons, Dragons, Nerds, Dirts, Ghouls, Giants, Vampires, Zombies, and Other Curiosa . . . , by Lee J. Ames. Doubleday, 1983.

Follow a few instructions and draw all these creatures that Ames has drawn and named, like Murt the Dirt and Quicksilver or Dracula and John Henry.

Drawing from Nature, by Jim Arnosky. Lothrop, 1982.

The rich variety of subjects for drawing comes from four sources: water, land, plants, and animals. You'll need a pencil and drawing pad—along with sharp eyes to see and wonder at what can be found in nature to draw. Arnosky tells you how he did each of his drawings to get the effect he wanted so that you can do the same.

Ed Emberley's Big Red Drawing Book. Little, 1987.

Emberley has a neat way of telling you what to draw. He starts with an empty square or a circle, tells you how large to make it and whether to fill in anything to make it look solid, and teaches you the order in which to put these shapes together to make a picture. The basic drawings turn into stylistic, holiday-oriented, lighthearted animals, people, and things.

How to Draw Monsters! by Rich Buckler. Solson, 1986.

The three-part arrangement is interesting: classic like Dracula, mythological like troll, and made-up monsters like hobgoblins. Also the large number of monsters is startling—some you probably don't know. After you get past looking, start drawing with the help of the short, often humorous directions, which tell you what to emphasize in order to be successful. This book is useful for both artists and nonartists, because it is almost an illustrated dictionary of monsters.

Just Look . . . a Book about Paintings, by Robert Cummings. Scribner, 1979.

The author soon asks quite a few questions, which you are expected to answer, sometimes using hints but mostly just looking at famous paintings, which are in color and properly captioned. This method teaches you a lot about composing a picture to accomplish your purpose and also about using color, shading, lighting, and real or unreal things, people, or animals. The artists whose pictures are shown in this book lived in four different centuries, and many subjects and styles are represented in their paintings. (The expected answers are given at the end of the book.)

Linnea in Monet's Garden, by Christina Bjork. Farrar, 1985.

Mr. Bloom, a gardener, is Linnea's upstairs neighbor; and they both love flowers—sufficiently to decide to visit Claude Monet's home and garden outside Paris. They take photographs, and Linnea sketches *one* water lily because she thinks it would be too hard to draw the whole pond, although she knows Monet did. Monet was a great impressionist artist who wanted to paint the sparkling, almost luminous, light of the changing sun reflecting on the water and everything else in his garden. They also manage to see the water lily rooms in a Paris museum, where Monet's masterpieces cover the walls.

Pencil, by Don Bolognese and Elaine Raphael. Watts, 1986.

The first pages are dedicated to praising the wonderfully available and useful drawing pencil. The beginning steps are shown immediately: how to choose and sharpen your pencil and select paper and how to use your finger, eraser, or water to create special effects. The varied techniques are illustrated, with an emphasis on structure and style. The last chapter takes a sketch from rough draft to finished form.

I Want a Good
Mystery to Solve

A Case for Jenny Archer, by Ellen Conford. Little, 1988.

After reading three mysteries in a row, Jenny becomes convinced that the neighbors moving in across the street are art thieves and decides to investigate. When she sees someone leaving the house with a painting, she calls 911. The police catch a thief but not Jenny's suspect.

The Case of the Baker Street Irregular, by Robert Newman. Atheneum, 1975.

Andrew Craigie and his guardian come to London after his aunt's death. His guardian is kidnapped, and now the kidnappers are after Andrew. He meets up with a girl, Screamer, and then with Sherlock Holmes. The chase is on! Experience London at the time of Holmes, as all pursue a great adventure.

The Case of the Cinema Swindle, by Terrance Dicks. Elsevier/Nelson, 1980.

Liz, Jeff, Mickey, and Dan form a group they call the Baker Street Irregulars. They are at the movies when Mickey discovers a fire set in the film-storage room of the local cinema. The four sleuths have a new mystery to solve, and they involve their friend Detective Day of the local police. Mickey is the youngest and most impulsive but manages to help in the hunt for the arsonist.

The Drackenberg Adventure, by Lloyd Alexander. Dutton, 1987.

Vesper Holly's aunt and uncle are invited by the Grand Duchess, ruler of Drackenberg, to attend her diamond jubilee. In 1873—

when Baedeker was *the* tourist guide, castles were homes, and the only transportation was the horse—Vesper and her aunt and uncle find themselves drawn into a neighboring country's plot to annex Drackenberg and to perpetrate an art theft. The three of them are taken prisoner and rescued by gypsies—with Vesper always resourceful enough to keep the balance of success tipped on her side.

Encyclopedia Brown and the Case of the Treasure Hunt, by Donald J. Sobol. Bantam, 1988.

Ten cases, one of them involving a cheater on a treasure hunt—that's a lot to solve even for Encyclopedia Brown, who is so clever, he usually has to ask only one question before he can solve the case. His father, who is chief of police in Idaville, and the neighborhood children rely on him. His real name is Leroy, and he hasn't raised the seat of his bicycle yet.

The Fourth Floor Twins and the Skyscraper Parade, by David A. Adler. Viking, 1987.

Identical twins Donna and Diane and their fourth-floor neighbors, the twins Gary and Kevin, search for the thief who stole the famous sculpture *Skyscraper Parade* from the museum. They are there when the theft is discovered but have to buy a postcard of it to see what the sculpture looked like! Now they know why the men they overheard were talking about wood and nails.

Incognito Mosquito Takes to the Air, by E. A. Hass. Random, 1986.

Incognito Mosquito, a private "insective" for bugs, is invited to be on a talk show with David Litterbug and appears with a paper bag over his head to protect his incognitohood. He recounts some tight scrapes with pirates, bank robbers, and book thieves and is challenged by the other two famous guests to solve a case on the air.

Mystery of the Dead Man's Riddle, by William Arden. Random, 1974.

Marcus (Dingo) Towne, widely known to be a millionaire, went about in old clothes and left a set of riddles in his will (but only one dollar to each of his four relatives). The majority of his estate will go to anyone who can find the treasure. The Three Investigators, a junior detective team, attempt to find Old Dingo's fortune, using six puzzling clues.

The View from the Cherry Tree, by Willo Davis Roberts. Atheneum, 1975.

Rob Mallory has lived nine of his eleven years next door to Mrs. Calloway and often—in fact, as much as possible—sits in the cherry tree that is closer to her house than his. Then suddenly it happens. The cat scratches the arms of a man in the house, as Mrs. Calloway falls out the window to her death. That is all that Rob sees. His sister's wedding distracts the whole family to such an extent that Rob finds himself alone with someone he suspects is the man with the scratched arms.

Where Are the Time Travel Books?

The Doll in the Garden, a Ghostly Story, by Mary Downing Hahn. Clarion, 1989.

Louisa is the owner of the doll that Ashley and her friend Kristi find buried in Miss Cooper's garden, but Louisa died seventy years ago. They never dream they will meet Louisa, anger Miss Cooper, understand the note that was buried with the doll, or relate their visits to the garden to see Louisa to the present time.

A Girl Called Boy, by Belinda Hurmence. Ticknor, 1982.

Blanche Overtha Yancey prefers to be called "Boy," whose letters stand for the initials of her name, and is ashamed that her ancestors were slaves, especially because they did not do something to stop being "pushed around," as she puts it. When a strange wishing stone transports her back in time to pre-Civil War days, she sees, since she's become a slave herself, that being a slave requires strength and courage.

Jeremy Visick, by David Wiseman. Houghton, 1981.

Matthew's visit to an old cemetery as part of a homework assignment leaves him haunted by the deaths of four of the Visick family who died in 1852 in a mining accident. He can't get them out of his mind, especially when the ghost of Jeremy Visick, who was Matthew's age when he died, visits him and invites him to cross through time and come work in the copper mines with them.

The People in Pineapple Place, by Anne Lindbergh. Harcourt, 1982.

August begins to lose that new-kid-in-town feeling and to have some fun after he meets April and the other kids about his age from Pineapple Place. The only problem is that no one else can see them, and Pineapple Place is not known to exist in Washington, D.C. They come from another place and another time. (They have been going to school for forty-three years already.) August suspects that their next stop will be Chicago, where he has a friend.

The Root Cellar, by Janet Lunn. Scribner, 1981.

When is life among people, places, or events of the past a comfort? Rose accidentally discovers not only the doors of an old root cellar but also the exact moment when they will open, allowing her to go back to Civil War times. She is convinced she would like to live in that time period rather than return to the Canadian relatives who agreed to take her when her other relatives died. She will always remember Susan, her best friend, and Will, a boy who awakens thoughts of marriage. The scenes of the war; her trip with Susan to find Will, dead or alive; and learning about the differences between her and her friends culminate in Rose's decision to come home.

Time at the Top, by Edward Ormondroyd. Parnassus, 1963.

Who would ever dream that an elevator in their apartment house could take them into the past? Not Susan, but that's what happened on a day when nothing went right. However, once there (1881) in a garden, she meets Victoria, her brother Robert, and mother, who is a widow in financial distress. In order to help her, the three hunt for and find a treasure, which also gives Susan proof of her journey back into time that she uses to convince her father he should make the trip.

Voices after Midnight, by Richard Peck. Delacorte, 1989.

When Californians Chad, Luke, Heidi, and their parents spend two weeks in a rented house in New York City one summer, they experience more than culture shock—they find themselves able to move back in time and become involved in the problems of the family that lived there during the blizzard of 1888 and whose descendants currently own the house. Once home in California, their dad consults the family Bible and discovers that the people in the 1880s are his cousins.

I Saw It. Do You Have the Book?

Across Five Aprils, by Irene Hunt. Follett, 1964.

From potato-planting time in April of 1861 when he is ten, Jethro experiences aspects of the war that has divided the country. He hears the arguments over whether it is human or economic issues that are causing the war and watches the enlistment of his brothers and best friend. This leaves the farmwork almost wholly to him and his sister, especially when their mother is taking care of their father, who becomes ill as other men threaten him and try to force him to choose sides after his sons end up on opposing sides. No wonder Jethro writes to Mr. Lincoln—and receives a reply. The president's response helps, but it is five long years until April, when the guns cease firing. Jethro awaits the end with high hopes—only to find it a cruel time when questions arise as to why war was fought in the first place and what will be worthwhile to do now that it is over.

How the Grinch Stole Christmas, by Dr. Seuss. Random, 1957.

Perhaps you like a Christmas book in summer. Certainly the Grinch's poor attitude toward the holiday and the Whos' reaction to the Grinch result in a clash that brings a spirit of friendliness we can appreciate all year.

Jane of Lantern Hill, by L. M. Montgomery. Bantam, 1989.

When Jane is twelve, her father asks her to come to Prince Edward Island for the summer. She does not want to leave her mother and is totally surprised when she likes her up-to-then unknown father and his house, in which she learns to sew, cook, and clean. School in Toronto and life with her mother in her grandmother's aristocratic, wealthy home are bearable only because she expects to stay with her father every summer. Her aunt scares Jane with the news that her father may remarry, and Jane arrives early the third summer seeking the truth and perhaps a reconciliation of her parents.

Pippi Longstocking, by Astrid Lindgren. Viking, 1950.

Certainly, Pippi is an unusual nine-year-old. She is probably an orphan, but she still has hopes that her father, a sea captain, did not drown when he was washed overboard. She brings Mr. Nilsson, a monkey, and a suitcase full of gold coins from the ship when she moves into the house her father owned. She buys a horse and begins an unusual life style that does not include school or an orphanage but does include adventures in a hollow tree, on a picnic, and at the circus with her neighbors Annika and Tommy Settergren. In her own unique way she wears out two burglars learning to dance the schottische, and she upsets Mrs. Settergren's coffee party with a combination of ship protocol and conversation full of exaggerations. She also saves two children from a burning building with her knowledge of ropes and knots. She has enormous physical strength, acts illogically at times, is extremely generous, and thinks life should be fun.

Ralph S. Mouse, by Beverly Cleary. Morrow, 1982.

Ryan and his mother, who is the housekeeper, live at a motel, as does Ralph S. (for Smart) Mouse, who has learned to talk from watching television. Ralph has a motorcycle, which he rides in the lobby of the motel at night. Matt the handyman and Ryan are the only humans who know this, and they are protective. When he and his motorcycle are threatened by other mice, Ralph decides that going to school with Ryan is a good way out. Ryan's class accidentally becomes involved in the Great Mouse Exhibit, from which they all learn, including Ralph; and we get both sides of the arguments, dangers, publicity, and rewards associated with it. The motorcycle is broken but replaced—with a sports car—and Ralph practices what he learned: Mice who want to ride must line up and take their turn. Ralph is pleased, too, because he knows their tails are safer in the car than on a motorcycle.

Sarah, Plain and Tall, by Patricia MacLachlan. Harper, 1985.

Anna's and Caleb's mother dies when Caleb is one day old. Now their father has placed a newspaper advertisement for a wife. Sarah Wheaton writes from Maine that she will come by train and that she is plain and tall. After she arrives, they learn she is also strong and independent and can sing. Only one question remains: Will she stay?

The Secret Garden, by Frances Hodgson Burnett. Dell, 1962.

Mary Lennox and Colin Craven are cousins about the same age. Each is lonely and can count the people she or he likes on one hand (and the number who like them is even smaller). Circumstances bring them together at Misselthwaite Manor, a one-hundred-room house on the moors in England. Mary meets Dickon, a brother of her housemaid, who's good with people, plants, and creatures, and Ben Weatherstaff, a gardener, who says his only friend is a robin. Mary finds the secret garden, and it becomes a means of restoring health to Mary and Colin, who need exercise in the fresh air and hearty food. They and Dickon work in the garden that has been locked for ten years and bring its plants to life in the spring and summer, trying to keep it all a secret to surprise Colin's father when he returns. He closed the garden when his wife died after an accident there, and he shuns the sight of Colin, who has lived as an invalid with the fear he will die very young.

I Want Something
Fun to Do!

Cat's Cradle, Owl's Eyes: A Book of String Games, by Camilla Gryski.
   Morrow, 1984.
   With just a piece of string and your own two hands you can
have lots of fun. You can play games like cat's cradle with a friend,
trick someone by trapping his hand in your string, or just make
interesting designs, like a "winking eye" or a "cup and saucer."
Diagrams and easy-to-follow instructions will get you started.

The Cat's Elbow and Other Secret Languages, collected by Alvin
   Schwartz. Farrar, 1982.
   Pig Latin is one of the best-known of the secret languages; but,
if you prefer, you can learn to speak Ziph, Kinyume, and several
other languages by following the directions in this book. The Cat's
Elbow is a German secret language; Ku comes from the children of
the Russian city of Chernovsty; and Sa-La was used by children in
Amoy, China, a hundred years ago. Oodgay Ucklay!

Devilish Bets to Trick Your Friends, by E. Richard Churchill. Sterling,
   1985.
   If you like fooling people, dare your friends to remove a dollar
bill from beneath an upside-down bottle (without touching the bottle), predict the date on a concealed coin, or even have them take
a simple reading test. When they fail each bet, you can be an angel
and amaze them with the devilishly easy solution!

How to Make Pop-Ups, by Joan Irvine. Morrow, 1987.
   With illustrated instructions, common materials and tools, and

your own great ideas, you are on your way to push, pull, pop out, fold and fit in, and turn creations. If you need a cutting blade, ask an adult to help. Try making the old-fashioned zoo or pet shop.

The Paper Airplane Book, by Seymour Simon. Viking, 1971.

Find out more about the forces of lift, thrust, drag, and gravity that keep airplanes in the air and learn the names and functions of the parts of a plane—the ailerons, flaps, stabilizers, and elevators—so you can design and make a variety of paper airplanes.

Secret Spaces, Imaginary Places: Creating Your Own Worlds for Play, by Elin McCoy. Macmillan, 1986.

Learn to make castles, tunnels, and other secret spaces out of easily found materials, like cardboard boxes or blankets. There are also instructions for more elaborate structures, like treehouses, snow caves, playhouses, and puppet stages. The sky's the limit! You can even make a spaceship!

Steven Caney's Kids' America, by Steven Caney. Workman, 1978.

This book will keep you busy for a year if you want it to! Make a scarecrow or soap, build a toy or a bird feeder, twist your tongue with tangled twisters or tell a fortune, or hold a garage sale and learn ways to save the money you take in! After you try all the different ideas contained in this 414-page book, you'll need a rest.

I Need That One about When the Weather's All Messed Up

Bartholomew and the Oobleck, by Dr. Seuss. Random House, 1949.

The king is tired of the four things that fall from the sky, and despite advice from Bartholomew that the sky is not his and is best left alone, the king summons his magicians who make oobleck to tumble down on everyone. Oobleck is green, it grows, and it's gooey-gummy. Not until the king is made helpless by oobleck does he pay any attention to Bartholomew. A king *never* says "I'm sorry!" However, this one does, and things settle back down to the four things that fall from the sky.

The Dark Is Rising, by Susan Cooper. Atheneum, 1973.

Will Stanton makes a wish for snow to fall on his eleventh birthday, and his wish comes true; but when Farmer Dawson gives him a strange iron ornament, he prophesies that the day will be beyond imagining! Will finds he is selected to join the Old Ones who fight the forces of evil, the Rider on the black horse, and the rocks. Merriman Lyon is his guide, and Will's task is to stop the snow and cold and to release the country from the Dark.

Dr. Dredd's Wagon of Wonders, by Bill Brittain. Harper, 1987.

To break the drought, the citizens of Coven Tree can be counted on to do almost anything, and a simple deal with Dr. Dredd, who will provide the services of Bufu, Miracle Boy of the East, also known as the Rainmaker, seems the most immediate solution. Ellen McCabe finds Bufu, who is really an orphan named Calvin Huckabee, hiding in the barn, trying to escape Dr. Dredd's beatings. She and her mother protect him, as does Stew Meat, the keeper of the general store, until they can overcome Dr. Dredd's terrible powers.

The Drought on Ziax II, by John Morressy. Walker, 1978.

Toren Mallixxan was born in space, and his father is leader of the earth pioneers who live on Ziax II. Just as the Imbur, the forest people who live there, they are also searching for water. Without the sork to eat it, the orange grass is soaking up the water and growing out of control, and the sork have been killed off by the earthmen. Toren and his friend Rilmat go with the expedition to locate any remaining sork and bring them back to save the planet.

Hurricane, by David Wiesner. Clarion, 1990.

When a hurricane blows up, David and George first make sure their cat Hannibal is indoors, then settle down to enjoy the excitement of using candles and hurricane lamps when the electricity goes off. The most fun, however, is next morning, when they find a neighbor's elm tree blown down. The elm tree becomes a jungle, a sailing ship, a spaceship, and just a place to sit, until men come with chain saws and cut it up into pieces. The boys are very sad, but there's another storm coming up, and if the other elm falls, it will be in *their* yard!

The Lion, the Witch and the Wardrobe, by C. S. Lewis. Macmillan, 1950.

Lucy can still see the open door of the wardrobe through which she can always go to get back—as she crunches over the snow in a place Faun tells her is Narnia and always winter. Edmund, her brother who doesn't believe her, is the next one to visit Narnia; and he meets a great lady on a sledge (the White Witch) pulled by reindeer. Susan and Peter go, too; but it is Lucy who thinks they should stay, since Faun has been arrested by the White Witch for helping Lucy, a human. Spring surrounds Aslan, the king of the woods, and they join him, hoping to rescue Edmund from the White Witch. After the battle between the White Witch and Aslan, the four stay on for a year enjoying the beach, returning to explain four coats that are missing from the wardrobe.

Noah and the Ark, story by Geraldine McCaughrean. Ideals, 1989.

Although his sons, his wife, and his friends all are unconvinced, Noah believes God's warning that there will be a great flood and builds an ark as God instructs him. Then he gathers two of each animal into the ark, and the rain starts. After forty days and nights of rain, the sun comes out, and at last the ark and its occupants find dry land and a promise from God that there will be no more floods to destroy the earth.

Do You Have That Book That Our Teacher Read to Us Last Week?

Half Magic, by Edward Eager. Harcourt, 1954.

Jane is the oldest child; Mark is the only boy; Katherine is a comfort to her mother, her mother says; but Martha, the youngest, is difficult. The approaching summer awakens in them a longing for excitement—for something magical—and the unexpected possibility of fulfilling this wish rests with Jane and a nickel she finds. Mark is skating with the nickel in his shoe, where Jane had put it, when he wishes for all four of them to be on a desert island. They definitely know the nickel is magic—but only half magic—since they arrive in a desert but not on an island. They learn from their experiences, however; and all, including their mother, participate in wishing until the charm is used up. Jane saves the nickel—just in case.

King of the Wind, by Marguerite Henry. Rand McNally, 1948.

The ancestry of Man o' War, also called Big Red, goes back more than two hundred years to a gold-tinged reddish bay horse called the Godolphin Arabian or Sham, which Agba, a slave boy in the royal stables in Morocco, takes care of. When Agba accompanies Sham, which the sultan has chosen to be presented to the king of France as a gift, he happily accepts the sultan's charge to take care of the horse for as long as the horse shall live. Until the preparations begin for the journey to France, no one except the chief of the grooms knows that Agba is a mute, but when the sultan finds this out he is all the more pleased for no secrets will escape. Agba and Sham stay together despite some bad experiences but attain recognition for Sham as King of the Wind in racing; and Sham is the source of the vitality that made Man o' War the greatest racer of his time.

My Side of the Mountain, by Jean George. Dutton, 1959.

No one has lived on the old Gribley farm for a hundred years, and Sam Gribley has to ask a librarian to help him locate it. It is his intent to live there—to make a house and to live off the land. The house, he decides, will take the form of a tree: not a tree house but a hollowed-out trunk. Will it be sufficient for a winter home and will he be proficient enough in gathering and hunting his food? His companion is Frightful, a falcon; a *few* people wander by, and he goes to town a *few* times. These encounters lead to the visit of a reporter, with whom he strikes a deal to avoid publicity *if* possible. The big surprise is when his family decides to join him permanently and build a house—until he is eighteen and can do as he pleases, which is only a few years away.

Redwall, by Brian Jacques. Philomel, 1986.

The mice built the abbey of Redwall; and for as long as anyone can remember, it has been a place of peace, protecting and healing the animals in the surrounding area. When Cluny the Scourge and his army of rats want to take it over as their headquarters and steal everything inside, it is the youngest, least likely mouse, Matthias, who seeks the ancient sword and allies himself with some of the other creatures to defend Redwall. They use interesting tactics to save their precious place.

The Sign of the Beaver, by Elizabeth George Speare. Houghton, 1983.

Matt is to guard the cabin while his father goes to get the rest of the family. An old Indian who rescues him wants Matt to teach his grandson to read, but Attean doesn't want to learn. Matt learns from them; and when they move their village, they would have taken him with them. He hopes his own family will return; and he stays and waits, more able to take care of himself now.

Stone Fox, by John Reynolds Gardiner. Crowell, 1980.

Only Willy seems to think he will win the sled dog race, and only Willy seems to be unaware that winning is probably impossible. The prize money from the race quite possibly will bring his grandfather back to an interest in life for which he is still physically able.

The crowd is large at the race between ten-year-old Willy with his one-dog sled and Stone Fox, a previous Indian winner with five Samoyeds. The crowd is silent at the finish of the five-mile race when Willy's dog Searchlight drops dead a hundred yards from winning.

Author-Title Index

Subject Index

Frances Laverne Carroll is professor emeritus, School of Library and Information Studies, University of Oklahoma (Norman). She and Mary Meacham have collaborated on several books, beginning with *The Library at Mount Vernon* in 1977. Carroll taught children's literature and initiated a course in international children's literature based on her travels and interest in the International Youth Library, children, and children's books.

Mary Meacham is currently a scientific librarian at a federal government research library. Previously, she taught children's literature and worked as a school librarian. Her dissertation compared four well-known children's book review journals over a sixty-year period, and she has written a book on sources of information about children's books for librarians and teachers as well as several articles on library science themes.